BASEBALL
JUST FOR KIDS

Skills, Strategies and Stories
to Make You a Better Ballplayer

Jerry Kasoff

Grand Slam Press, Inc.
2 Churchill Road
Englewood Cliffs, NJ 07632

ISBN 0-9645826-7-8

LCCN 95-79529

First printing 1996

Although the author and publisher have made every effort to ensure the accuracy and completeness of information contained in this book, we assume no responsibility for errors, inaccuracies, omissions, or any inconsistency herein. Any slights of people, places, or organizations are unintentional.

Acknowledgements
With thanks and appreciation to all the coaches, officials, and especially the kids (past and present) of the Englewood Cliffs Little League, whose sportsmanship and love of the game inspired me to write this book.

Photo Acknowledgements
Willie Stargell and Bill Mazeroski, courtesy of Pittsburg Pirates Baseball Club; Roger Clemens, courtesy of Boston Red Sox; Babe Herman and Pete Reiser, courtesy of Los Angeles Dodgers Inc.; All other pro players, courtesy of National Baseball Library and Archive in Cooperstown, NY. Front and back cover photos: Bob Tringali, Sports Chrome, Inc., Cliffside Park, NJ. All photos contained within are protected by copyright and are not reprintable without the express permission of the owner.

Attention: Educational Institutions, Organizations and Corporations: Quantity discounts are available on bulk purchases of this book for educational purposes, gifts, or fund raising. Special books or book excerpts can also be created to fit specific needs. For information, please contact our Special Sales Department, 2 Churchill Road, Englewood Cliffs, NJ 07632, (201) 541-9181.

Table of Contents

Introduction

The game of baseball belongs to kids. It's *your* game. You learn it when you're six or seven and play it until twelve or thirteen. Then on to high school and other interests. You probably won't swing a bat very often after that.

The heart and soul of baseball is on the sandlots and Little League fields. Kids play for the pure fun of it. Your spirit blesses the game with its magic. It will be part of you for the rest of your life.

I love kids' baseball. They told me I can't play it any more—some nonsense about an age limit. So I've been doing the next best thing: coaching Little League baseball in a wonderful place called Englewood Cliffs, New Jersey. I started in 1980 and I'm going to do it forever!

I've written this book *just for kids* to read. You can let your coach or your parents borrow it if you want (they might learn something too). But it's your book. It speaks directly to you.

Most kids really don't know much about baseball. They play on raw talent and gut reactions alone. Your coach's time is limited. He or she can't possibly devote enough attention to each one of you to perfect your style or to teach the finer points of the game.

That's why this book will help you. Each chapter teaches a different piece of the game. You'll learn how to hit, field, run, etc., and watch your skills improve. Even more important, you'll learn about strategies, rules, famous players and memorable events. You'll *understand* baseball and enjoy it as never before.

A few bases I must touch:

- *Righty/Lefty*: Parts of the book are written for a right-handed player. If you're a lefty, be a switch-reader (read 'left' for 'right' and vice versa).

- *Boy/Girl*: Many girls play kids' baseball. Some are stars, and some simply love the game. I hope they'll forgive me for writing in the masculine gender. It's awkward to keep alternating from "he" to "she," or to refer to each of you as an "it." Just remember that the game of baseball is for both boys *and* girls.

- *Little League/Major League*: Little Leaguers and their ballparks are both built much smaller than their major league counterparts. Because of this, many rules and strategies are different. Don't be surprised when you see a pro do something you were taught not to do. You may both be right.

- *Coach/Author*: Coaches sometimes disagree with each other on methods and strategies. Your coach may have some ideas that differ from what you read here. When this happens, it's okay to mention the difference to him. But *always* do what your coach tells you to.

- *Records*: You'll read some interesting facts and important records that every well-informed fan should know. Regarding the season and career records that follow:

  — They cover only baseball's modern era, beginning in 1900.

  — Official totals include only regular season games. Playoff and World Series records are always a separate category.

If you want to get the most out of this book, there are two "musts":

  — You must take a moment to *think* about what you read. It's important to understand the reasons for the strategies and styles of play. If you understand, you won't forget.

  — You must keep practicing what you've read. *Practice* makes perfect.

If you think and you practice, I *promise*:

  — You will become a much better baseball player.

  — You will have a lot more fun playing the game.

I wish you good luck and good times in kids' baseball. May it reward you with memories you'll treasure for the rest of your life.

1

Baserunning

Knowing how to run the bases will win you more games than anything else you can do.

Bold baserunning makes things happen. It creates ways to score runs you wouldn't otherwise have scored—runs that could be the difference between winning and losing.

When You Hit the Ball

Always:

- Be off at the crack of the bat. As soon as you make contact, you are a runner.

- Run *everything* out, full speed ahead. Never assume you will be out, no matter how easy the play seems to be. *There is no such thing as a sure out.*

Willie Mays was my favorite player. One time he hit a high, easy pop-up. I'll never forget watching him run so hard he was at third base by the time the shortstop caught the ball. Willie knew he'd be out, but he couldn't play any other way.

Running to First Base

When You Hit a Grounder to the Infield

- Don't watch the ball. Don't even look at it or it will slow you down. It doesn't help you to know where the ball is. You only care about beating the throw to first.

- As soon as you hit the ball, you're in a race. Put a rocket in your pocket and zoom down the basepath.

- Keep your eyes on the bag all the way. Run on the foul side of the line.

- Overrun first base. Don't ease up or slide or jump at the base or come to a screeching halt there. Accelerate your speed and run *through* the base (but make sure you touch it).

  — You are allowed to overrun first base. You can't be tagged out provided you return to first right away and don't make any move toward second.

- After overrunning, turn toward the infield side as you return to first. That way you can break toward second if there is an opportunity.

- If you do break for second and then change your mind, hurry back to first before you are tagged out.

When You Hit the Ball to the Outfield

- Watch the ball, and watch your first base coach too.

Overrun First Base

- About five feet before first base, veer slightly right of the baseline and circle toward first base, *always at full speed*. You want to be able to round the base and make a move toward second. Circling like this lets you sharpen the angle and shorten the distance to second (otherwise your momentum will force you to run wide and toward the outfield).

- Try to land with your right foot near the inside corner of first base (the corner nearest to the pitcher), and push off hard toward second base.

- Always make a big turn toward second. Decide whether to go for it as you round first base.

- It's not a bad idea to fake going to second, in order to draw a throw there. Sometimes the ball will get away and you can swipe an extra base or two.

Tagging up

- You *must* understand this rule:

  If a batted ball is caught by a fielder before it touches the ground, a baserunner must touch his base after the catch is made. He can then "tag up" and try to go on to the next base.

- If the runner leaves his base too soon, he will be "doubled off" (out) if a fielder with the ball touches that base (or tags the runner) before the runner gets back to it.

- If he "tags up" after the catch, he will be safe at the next base unless he is tagged with the ball before he gets there.

What Should You Do If You're on Base?

- *On an Outfield fly*
  - Runners at first and second can go part way toward the next base, and wait to see if the ball is caught.
  - A runner on third should stay at the base and be ready to dart home as soon as the catch is made.

Be Ready to Tag up on the Catch

- *On An Infield Pop-Up*
  - — Take a short lead and see if the ball is caught.
  - — Don't take a lead if the pop-up is near your base.
  - — The infielders may have left a base uncovered after the catch. Maybe you can tag up.

- *On a line drive* that is caught in the infield, hustle right back to your base.

9

- *On any foul ball,* stay on your base and be ready to tag up if you can.

Sliding

You can't learn how to slide from reading a book. You've got to be shown how to do it correctly by your coach or instructor.

There are some very basic points you must know:

- Once you have begun to slide, go through with it. Never hesitate or pull back or slow down or change your mind after your slide is under way.

- *Never slide head first.* You can suffer crippling injuries to your head, neck, back, hands, etc., in a head-first slide. I know the pros do it, but they are professionals, they practice it a lot, they know how to protect themselves—and yet even they sometimes get hurt. You are playing youth baseball. Being put out or losing a game is not a tragedy. Don't risk an injury that could ruin your life.

- When you slide:
  - Keep your eyes on the bag.
  - Begin your slide several feet before the bag.
  - Don't jump into the slide.
  - Relax your legs.
  - Stay low to the ground as you start the slide.
  - Keep your hands up as you slide.

- Keep your foot on the base after the slide. The baseman may swipe at you with a second tag as you get up. Stay on the base until the umpire has called "time out."

Hands up, Eyes on the Bag

- Look for the ball. If it has gotten away, scramble back to your feet and take another base.

- *When in doubt, slide!*

Stealing a Base

- Once you begin your steal, the first rule is: Go! Turn on the juice. Never pause or slow down until you reach the base.

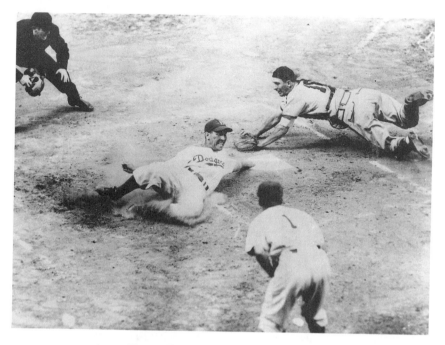

Pete Reiser Steals Home

- If a throw is made, *always slide.*

- When stealing second base, don't watch the catcher. Keep your eye on the base and on the fielder taking the throw.

- At second base, go part way down to third on *every* pitch. Watch the ball. Watch the coach. Be on your toes and quick to react.

- To steal home, begin to run a few steps at full speed just as the ball crosses the plate. This gives you momentum and puts you closer to home.

  — If the pitch gets away from the catcher, you now have a huge advantage if you decide to break for it.

The Most Important Base Stealing Records

- *Most Stolen Bases in a Season:* Ricky Henderson (A's) stole 130 bases in 1982.
- *Most Career Stolen Bases:* Ricky Henderson had 1,149 as of the end of the 1995 season.
- *Most Stolen Bases In a Game:* Eddie Collins (A's) stole 6 bases twice during the 1912 season. Otis Nixon (Braves) did it once in 1991.
- *Most Steals of Home in a Season:* Pete Reiser (1946 Dodgers) and Rod Carew (1969 Twins) each stole home seven times.
- *Most Career Steals of Home:* Ty Cobb (Tigers) did it 35 times.
- *Most Consecutive Successful Stolen Bases:* Vince Coleman (Cardinals) stole 50 straight before being nabbed (1989-1990).
- *Only Player Ever to Steal 40 Bases and Hit 40 Homers:* Jose Canseco (A's) in 1988.

— If the pitch is cleanly caught, watch out for the pick-off throw and be ready to return to third (or perhaps do a 'delayed steal,' as described below).

There Are Many "Trick" Steals You Can Try

— When you walk, run to first base. See if anyone is covering second. If the fielders are asleep or if the pitch has gotten away from the catcher, don't stop at first but scamper right on down.

— With a runner on third, you might steal second without even drawing a throw. But don't take it for granted. Run, don't loaf. If you steal, *go on the first pitch.*

— Be alert. You might just keep going to second when you walk with a runner on third.

— Be aware. With two out they are more likely to make a play on you. Your out would end the inning. Try to avoid being tagged until the runner on third has crossed the plate.

— "Delayed Steals": The runner goes part way down the line after the pitch. As the catcher returns the ball, he breaks for the next base instead of going back. This is outrageous and it can drive your opponents berserk.

— Whenever a throw is made on a steal, all other runners should watch to see if they can advance.

• Be a thief! Stay alert! Seize the moment! There will be many opportunities to steal. That extra base may be just the edge you need for a win.

The dumbest steal ever, believe it or not, was attempted by Babe Ruth. It was the climactic moment of the 1926 World Series. Game seven, bottom of the ninth, two out, Cardinals holding onto a 3-2 lead over the Yankees.

The Babe was potbellied and far from swift. He drew a walk. The power clean-up hitter (Bob Meusel) came up to bat, with Lou Gehrig on deck.

To everyone's amazement, Ruth suddenly broke for second. He was out by a mile. It was the last out of the Series.

There had been no signal to steal. The Babe never could explain what made him try it.

Infield Fly Rule

- Here's what you must remember about this rule:

  When the umpire calls "Infield Fly Rule":
  — You are *not forced* to go to the next base if the ball is dropped.
  — Otherwise, the ball is played like any other infield pop-up. You may try to go to the next base at your own risk; and you can be "doubled off" your base if the ball is caught.

- The Infield Fly Rule is not complicated at all. It is simply this:
  — If there are less than two out; **and**
  — If there are runners at first and second, or first, second and third;

  Then on any fly ball that can be readily caught by an infielder, the batter is automatically out (whether or not the ball is caught).

  Since the batter is automatically out, this removes the force on the baserunners and they can remain at their own bases.

- The umpire must call the Infield Fly Rule.

- A line drive or a bunt is not an infield fly.

- If you understand the reason for the rule, it makes sense. The runners would not run on a pop-up, for fear of being "doubled off." However, if not for the Infield Fly Rule, they would be forced to advance if an infielder intentionally let the ball drop. When there are two runners on base, it would be an easy double play every time.

Caught in a Rundown

Trapped between the bases! How embarrassing! What to do?

- Keep the rundown going as long as you can. Fake moves! Draw throws! With every throw they may bungle it and let you escape.

- If you're really in a pickle (this is a *last* resort), be a clown. Dance around! Make faces! Taunt them! But keep moving. The fielders may lose their concentration and let you wiggle out of it. No kidding—I've seen this work. Get them to laugh at you, and you'll have the laugh on them. (If you do try this, don't get so caught up in the festivities that you lose your concentration and defeat your own purpose.)

- Don't run outside the baselines. You must stay within three feet of the line between the bases, or you're out.

- With other runners on base, prolong the rundown to give them a chance to advance. With two out and a runner on third, try to avoid the tag until he crosses the plate so the run will count.

- When you make it safely to a base, you're not done. Check out the next base. Is anyone covering it? If not, be aggressive and go for it.

- When all else fails and you're a dead duck, don't just stand there to be tagged. Scoot to either base to draw a throw. Pick the base with the weakest fielder. Who knows—you could get lucky.

Dos and Don'ts of Baserunning

Do

- Be Alert
- Be Bold
- Be Clever
- On every pitch and every play, look for a way to take another base.
- Make the defense throw as much as possible. The more they throw, the more likely they will throw it away. Keep them confused and off balance. Surprise them. For instance:
    - Take big turns rounding a base. If they throw behind you, maybe take off for the next base.
    - Fake a dash to the next base, to draw a throw.
    - Keep on going to the next base when it's not expected.
    - Watch the runner ahead of you. Stay one base behind him. If he goes for an extra base, you should too. The play will usually be on him.
- Be aware of the defense's boners and blunders. For instance:
    - Is their attention turned away from you? Did they leave the next base uncovered? Have they thrown to a wrong base?
- Know where the ball is at all times.
- Know the game situation while you're on base. How many are out? Are you forced? Are there other runners on base? What is the score? Think *before* each pitch

what you will do on a fly, or a grounder, or a wild pitch. If you wait to figure it out after the ball is hit, it will be too late.

- Be sure to touch each base.
- Before each pitch, get into the "ready to run" position:
  — One foot against the base.
  — Lean forward with your weight on the ball of your foot.
  — Be set to drive off.
- Run down a few steps on every pitch as soon as the ball crosses the plate.
- If you're forced, you must run on a ground ball. Don't hesitate—GO!
- If you're not forced and a grounder is hit to an infielder, fake a few steps toward the next base to see if he throws to that base or to first. If the throw is to first, you must judge whether you can then advance on the throw. (A runner at second should always go to third on a grounder hit to the right side of the infield.)
- With two out, run on anything (as soon as the ball is hit). With less than two out, think about tagging up on a fly ball.
- Before the game, and between innings, observe the catcher and outfielders. Know where you can take advantage of a weak arm.
- Run to first and to home just outside the foul line (in foul territory).
- Your league may have a rule that you must slide on a play at home or be automatically out. Check this.

Get Set to Run

- If a base is kicked loose, run as if it were still in its correct position. Don't chase after the base.

- Watch the third base coach (not the ball) after you round second. He can see the whole field. He'll signal you whether to stop, slide, or keep on going.

- Rounding second or third base is much like rounding first.
    - Make a slight circling move to the right as you near the base.
    - Keep going at full speed.

— Hit near the inside corner of the base.

— Lean your body weight into the turn (toward the mound).

— Push off hard toward the next base.

— Try to make a square turn. Don't run wide outside the baseline. It will cost you precious time.

Don't

• Don't step off your base unless you know where the ball is. Never, never step off a base if a fielder innocently tells you to. (Guess what's in his glove?) Don't fall for the "hidden ball trick," the oldest trick in the game.

• Don't get hit by a batted ball. (You'll be out.)

• Don't pass the runner in front of you on the basepaths. (You'll be out.)

• Don't run more than three feet outside a direct line between the bases to avoid a tag. (You'll be out.)

• Don't interfere with a fielder attempting to make a play. (You'll be out.)

• Don't leave your base before the pitch reaches the plate. (You won't be out, but the umpire will nullify any advantage you gained by leaving early.)

Three Men on a Base—The "Daffiness Dodgers"

Kids are not the only ones who can blunder on the basepaths. Even the pros do it.

Brooklyn's "Daffiness Dodgers" of the 1920s may have been the most inept team of all time. They certainly were the funniest. Their top clown was Babe Herman, a good hitter whose strong bat was not matched by his brain.

Babe once came to bat with the bases loaded (Hank De Berry on third, Dazzy Vance on second, and Chick Fewster on first). Babe hit a hard line drive off the center field wall, and DeBerry scored from third. Dazzy got off to a slow start from second, and after rounding third he changed his mind and decided to go back. Chick got off to a good start from first and arrived at third base just as Dazzy was returning to it.

Meanwhile, Babe thundered around the bases. He was thrilled to slide into third with a triple. Then he looked up and, to his amazement, who did he find waiting there for him? Dazzy and Chick. The Dodgers had three men on the same base at the same time. It had never been done before (or since).

Babe Herman had "tripled into a double play." (Babe and Chick were both out when tagged; Dazzy, the lead runner, had the right to the base.) Babe's boner will never be forgotten, but as it turned out, his hit had driven in DeBerry with the game-winning run.

It became a joke in Brooklyn after that. Whenever a radio broadcaster announced "The Dodgers have three men on base," everyone would ask, "Which base?"

Babe Herman did some other wonderful things. Playing one day in the outfield, he lost a fly ball in the sun and it came down and hit him on the head. Another time, he hit a single and tripped over first base, falling flat on his face. He also stole third base with the bases loaded. Actually, he was a pretty good ballplayer, and definitely one of the most colorful who ever played the game.

Babe Herman

The Best and the Worst Baserunning

The Best

1946 World Series between the Cardinals and the Red Sox. Game seven. Bottom of the eighth inning. Two out. Score tied 3-3.

Cardinal Enos Slaughter reaches first on a single. Harry Walker then singles to left center, sending Slaughter to third. But Slaughter, galloping like a racehorse, rounds third. He sees Red Sox shortstop Johnny Pesky hesitate with the relay before throwing home. Slaughter turns it on. He keeps going and crosses the plate with the run that wins the World Series.

The Worst

1908 Pennant Race between the Giants and the Cubs. Crucial game at the end of the season. Bottom of the ninth. Two out. Score tied 1-1.

Giants have runners Fred Merkle on first and Moose McCormick on third. Batter Al Bridwell singles to center and Moose crosses the plate. It's the winning run, right? Wrong! Merkle thinks the game is won and joyfully runs off the field. He never touches second base. The Cubs appeal. Merkle is out; the run doesn't score, and the game remains tied.

What happened next? The crowd also thought the game was over, and they ran out onto the field. The season ended in a tie. A makeup game had to be played. This time the Cubs won, 4-2, for the National League pennant.

2

Batting

Hitting a baseball is the most difficult feat in any sport. The greatest batters in history made out more often than they hit safely. A .300 hitter today is paid millions, and he fails more than twice for every hit he gets.

It's even harder in kids' baseball. You stand closer to the pitcher (46 feet) than a major leaguer (60 feet). You've got to be quick.

So don't be discouraged if you don't smash the apple every time. Learn the fundamentals. Practice. You'll be amazed at what you can do.

When you bat, on every pitch, remember these things above all else:

Keep your eye on the ball all the way, from the moment it leaves the pitcher's hand until the moment it hits your bat. Don't look out or away. You should be looking at the ball even as you sock it.

Concentrate on making contact with the ball. Just meet the ball with a good stroke. Don't swing too hard.

Don't try to kill it. A well-timed swing will get you plenty of distance.

The Swing

This section tells you how to swing the bat. It is only a guide. You don't have to follow it exactly. Groove your own swing. Find the style that is right for you. But remember, these *are* the basics. Stick to them as closely as you comfortably can.

The Bat

• Use a bat that feels natural in your hands.

• Use a bat you can control.

• Too light is better than too heavy. A light bat gives your swing more speed and more power.

• One test to see if it's too heavy: Take the handle of the bat in one hand. Lift it, extend your arm, and point the bat straight out in front of you. Can you hold it steady?

The Grip

• Don't hold the bat back in the palm of your bands. Hold it and control it in your fingers.

• Begin by grasping the bat so that the middle knuckles of both hands are lined up with each other (more or less). Then lower the barrel of the bat to the ground. These knuckles should be pointing downward.

• That's the standard grip. You can vary it a bit until it feels comfortable and natural.

• Hold the bat firmly, but not too tightly.

The Right Grip Is Important

- You can choke up about an inch if it gives you better control. If you want to choke up more than that, don't. Take a lighter bat instead.

The Stance

Your Body

- Stand up straight. Relax.
- Tilt your upper body slightly forward from the waist.
- Head is straight up, facing the pitcher.
- Shoulders point at the pitcher.

Your Legs

- Feet are apart at shoulder width, even with each other, pointing at the plate.
- Knees are slightly bent, not stiff.
- Weight is on the balls of your feet. Don't stand flat-footed.

- Your weight should be almost even, but a bit more on the rear foot.

Your Arms

- Your arms and elbows must be *out away from your body*, so that you can swing freely.
- Your front arm is shoulder high and level to the ground.
- Pull your front upper arm back toward the catcher. You should now feel some tension at the shoulder. Your elbow points toward the plate (but level, not down).
- Your rear arm will find a comfortable position by itself. Just be sure to keep the elbow up and away from your ribs.

- This stance will pull your chin down toward the inside of your front shoulder. Your eyes are on the pitcher.

Your Hands

- Your hands are at shoulder height, slightly behind your rear shoulder.
- Don't hold your hands against your shoulder. Keep them out and free to move. Your front elbow should form an "L," not a "V."
- Cock your wrists a bit. The bat should point upward and slightly back. Don't wrap it around your neck.

Before the Pitcher Begins His Windup

- Relax. Don't stand there like a statue.
- Move the bat around. Take practice swings.
- Rock your body. Wiggle your toes. Step out of the box if you wish. Stay loose.

As the Pitcher Begins His Windup

- Set yourself. Get ready for the pitch.
- Don't move your head. Don't move your body. Don't move the bat. Don't move at all.
- Stay relaxed, not tense. Don't stiffen up.

The Stride

The stride begins by shifting your weight to your rear foot and moving the bat slightly back as you shift.

Begin this as soon as the pitcher starts his windup. It puts you into position early to move forward into the pitch. It gives you more time to complete your swing. If you wait until the ball approaches, it will go past you before you can bring the bat around.

Begin to stride early on *every* pitch. You won't know if it's a strike or a ball until it's too late.

Shifting Back

(Do this at the start of the windup)

- Begin your stride by transferring your weight to the inside of your rear leg.
- The leg doesn't move. Your body is going to push off from it.
- Your foot and knee lock into place.
- Your weight is on the ball of your foot.
- Your hips lock. They hardly turn at all.
- Your shoulders turn as your arms bring the bat farther around your back. (Bring it back level. Don't drop your elbows or shoulder.)
- *Don't lean back.* Your body stays upright. Your head doesn't move.

Stepping into the Ball

(Do this as the ball is released)

- Now step into the ball.
- As you do, *keep your body back behind the stride.*

- — Don't lean forward into the swing. Don't lunge at the ball.
- — Everything stays back. You will hit off your back foot.
- You step forward by pushing off your rear leg.
- Step toward the pitcher. Stride only about six inches.
- Your arms begin to bring the bat around into the swing. Don't start your swing until your foot is about to touch the ground.
- Your step lands on the ball of the foot, with the toes pointing at the pitcher.
- Remember to keep your body back.

The Swing

(Meet the Ball in Front of the Plate, Not Over the Plate)

- Keep your weight back and your eyes on the ball.

- Push off hard from your back foot and step into the pitch.

- Rotate your hips. They give your swing its power. Open them up so that your belly button faces the pitcher.

- Keep your head still and your eyes on the ball. The swing revolves around your hips and your head.

- Extend your arms as you whip the bat forward. Your front arm pulls the bat forward and leads the swing.

- Swing level, or even slightly downward.

- Don't drop your hands or your back shoulder as you swing. That will cause you to uppercut and you'll probably whiff at it.

- On a low pitch, bend your knees and drop your hands to meet it. Keep the swing level.

- Begin to uncock your wrists as the bat approaches the ball, not at the start of the swing. Your wrists should finish opening up just as the bat meets the ball.

- Swing hard. Feel as if you are hitting through the ball, not slapping at it.

- As you make contact, *your weight is still back* and you are hitting off your rear leg. Now you go into the follow-through.

The Follow-Through

- As you contact the ball, your rear leg pushes and transfers your weight forward.

- Your rear leg pivots and comes forward onto the toe.

- The momentum of your swinging arms carries your body forward and around.

- Follow through all the way. Don't hold back. Keep your bat high. Let your arms swing out and around so that the bat ends up behind you.

- After contact, your wrists roll over naturally.

- Don't let go of the bat. Hold onto it with both hands at the end of the swing.

Learning the Swing

- As you can see, the swing is made up of many parts. Try one part at a time. Get the feeling of it. Practice in front of a mirror, a parent, or a friend. Or check yourself out with a videotape.

- As you master each of the parts, put them together into a *slow* practice swing. Don't memorize all the parts. Practice the swing until you get the rhythm. Then you won't have to think about it—it will become natural to you.

- When you go into a slump (it will happen), recheck all the parts of your swing. You'll find the fault and get yourself back into the groove again.

Batting Pointers

- Stand toward the back of the plate (particularly with a fastball pitcher). It gives you a little more time to react to the pitch.

- Stand close to the plate, so you'll be able to reach a pitch over the outside. Be sure your bat is long enough.

- Await the pitch with your front arm level at shoulder height. Anything higher than your arm is out of the strike zone. Don't swing at it.

- Don't take a pitch if you're not ready. Step out of the batter's box before the pitcher begins his delivery.

- Know where the *strike zone* is. The ball must be:
  - — Over the plate.
  - — No higher than your armpit.
  - — No lower than the top of your knees.

- *Umpires often enlarge the strike zone.* They won't admit it, but they do. They don't widen it a lot, just a little bit. Umpires like to give the pitcher a break, especially if the kid is struggling with his control.

- *With two strikes, you must guard the plate!* Swing if the ball is close to the strike zone—you could be called out on a pitch that is a "ball!" Concentrate on making contact with the pitch, even if you only foul it off.

- With less than two strikes, don't swing at any pitch that fools you. But with two strikes, choke up and get the bat on the ball any way you can.

- An outside fastball is the most common pitch in kids' baseball. Expect it as you step to the plate. When it comes, you'll be ready for it.

- Get ahead in the count. It's a huge advantage.
  - — Swing at a good pitch. You might not get another one as good.
  - — Don't swing at a bad pitch. You're giving the pitcher a gift.

- At 3 and 0, let it go. Check with your coach for the okay to swing.

- Observe the pitcher as he warms up and while you're on deck. Get the feel of his pitches before you're up at bat.

- Take at least fifty practice swings with a heavier bat every day. (Do it *outside* the house!) It will strengthen your arms and groove your swing.

- When the runner on third steals home, step far back out of the batter's box and away from the throw. If you don't, it is interference and the runner will be called out.

- To duck an inside pitch, turn your head and shoulder around toward the catcher. (If you turn toward the pitch, you can get hit in the face.) Step back quickly or hit the dirt if you must.

- If you're constantly whiffing, you've got to concentrate on simply meeting the ball. Try this in practice or at a batting cage:
  — Eyes on the ball all the way.
  — Take a full but *easy* swing.
  — Try to hit the ball back only to the pitcher. When you start to make contact again, you can gradually begin to swing harder.

The Most Important Batting Records

Home Runs

- *Most Home Runs in a Season*: Roger Maris (Yankees) had 61 in 1961 (162 games). Babe Ruth (Yankees) had 60 in 1927 (154 games).

- *Most Career Home Runs*: Hank Aaron (Braves)—755.

   Babe Ruth had previously held the record (714). As the 1973 season ended, Aaron was one homer short, with 713. Can you imagine how he must have felt all winter long, waiting for his shot at the record? Hank wasted no time in 1974, hitting number 714 on opening day and number 715 a few days later.

   Hank Aaron is not only first in home runs. He is also the first name alphabetically of all who ever played major league baseball.

- *Most Home Runs in a Game*: Twelve players have hit four in one game. But only Lou Gehrig (Yankees), Rocky Colavito (Indians), and Mike Schmidt (Phillies) have done so in four consecutive times at bat.

- *Most Home Runs by a Team*: The 1961 Yankees had 240. Roger Maris had 61 and Mickey Mantle had 54.

- *Most Grand Slams in a Season*: Don Mattingly (Yankees)—six in 1987.

- *Most Career Grand Slams*: Lou Gehrig (Yankees)—23.

- *Most Consecutive Games Hitting a Home Run*: Eight.

   Dale Long (Pirates)—1956

   Don Mattingly (Yankees)—1987

   Ken Griffey, Jr. (Mariners)—1993

- *The Longest Home Run*: Mickey Mantle (Yankees) hit a towering blast out of Griffith Stadium, Washington, D.C., in 1953. The ball traveled 565 feet. That's almost the length of two football fields.

Hank Aaron Belting Number 715

Mickey Mantle

Hits

- *Most Hits in a Season*: George Sisler (St. Louis Browns) —257 in 1920.

- *Most Career Hits*: Pete Rose (Reds)—4256.

- *Longest Hitting Streak*: Joe Di Maggio (Yankees)—56 consecutive games in 1941.

Batting Average

- *Highest Batting Average in a Season*: Rogers Hornsby (Cardinals)—.424 in 1924.

- *Highest Career Batting Average*: Ty Cobb (Tigers)—.367.

- *Most Batting Titles*: Ty Cobb (Tigers)—12.

- *Highest Team Batting Average*: 1930 Giants—.319.
- *Last .400 Hitter*: Ted Williams (Red Sox)—.406 in 1941.
- — Trivia: No ballclub has ever won a pennant with a .400 hitter on the team.

Slugging Average

- *Highest Slugging Average in a Season*: Babe Ruth (Yankees)—.847 in 1920.
- *Highest Career Slugging Average*: Babe Ruth (Yankees)—.690.

Runs Batted In

- *Most RBI in a Season*: Hack Wilson (Cubs)—190 in 1930.
- *Most RBI in a Career*: Hank Aaron (Braves)—2297.

Runs

- *Most Runs Scored in a Season*: Babe Ruth (Yankees)—177 in 1921.
- *Most Career Runs Scored*: Ty Cobb (Tigers)—2245.

Baseball's Most Unforgettable Home Runs
"The Shot Heard 'Round The World"

In mid-August 1951, the Brooklyn Dodgers held a 13½-game lead over the New York Giants. They looked like a shoo-in. Dodger manager Charlie Dressen informed the press, "The Giants is dead."

Then the Giants began their "Miracle Run." Winning 39 of their last 47 games, they caught the Dodgers on the last day and forced a three-game playoff for the National League flag.

The teams split Games one and two. Game three was for all the marbles. Brooklyn held a 4-2 lead in the bottom of the ninth inning. The Giants were down in their last ditch. With runners on second and third, Brooklyn brought in their ace pitcher, Ralph Branca, to put out the fire. The batter, Bobby Thomson, already had a single and a double. Branca threw two pitches down the strike zone. The first one was called strike one. On the second one, Thomson smashed a hard line drive that was still rising as it crashed into the left field seats for the game-winning home run.

The Giants won the pennant! It was the most incredible finish in baseball history.

Babe Ruth Calls His Shot

In the 1932 World Series, bitter feelings ran high between the Yankees and the Cubs. Both dugouts hurled insults at each other. In Game three, Chicago fans also hurled garbage at Babe Ruth as he stepped to the plate.

Babe watched two called strikes whiz past him. He shouted something unprintable at his tormentors. Then he raised his bat and pointed to the center field bleachers.

In came the pitch and out went the ball over the fence where the Babe had pointed.

When asked later what he would have done if he'd struck out after calling his shot, Babe replied, "I never thought of that."

Babe Ruth

The World Series Ended on a Home Run

For the first time ever, in Game seven of the 1960 Series between the Yankees and Pirates. With the score tied in the bottom of the ninth, Pirate Bill Mazeroski belted one into the left field stands for the victory.

The 1993 World Series ended when Blue Jay Joe Carter homered in the ninth inning of Game six. The Blue Jays won that Series, 4 games to 2.

A Jubilant Bill Mazeroski Heads for Home

3

Bunting

Learn how to bunt. Not many kids do it well. But the bunt can be a powerful run-scoring weapon.

- It can advance a baserunner (sacrifice bunt).

- It can fluster the infielders. More errors are committed on bunts than on any other play.

- If you're not a strong hitter, or if you're up against a tough pitcher, it's a way to get your bat on the ball and beat out a hit.

- In kids' baseball, a well-placed bunt will get you on base more than half the time.

Learning to bunt is like learning to ride a bike. It seems difficult at first, but once you get the hang of it you can do it in your sleep.

There Are Two Kinds of Bunts

The Square Bunt:

- Turn on your front foot. Point the toes at the pitcher.

- Swing your back foot forward, even with the front one.

- Stay in the batter's box. Don't put your foot behind the plate.

- You are now facing the pitcher squarely.

The Square Bunt

The Pivot Bunt:

- Put your weight on your front foot. Point the toes at the pitcher.

- Don't move your back foot.

- Pivot your hips and knees around toward the pitcher.

The Pivot Bunt

- The back foot raises onto its toes as you pivot. Be ready to push off on it toward first base as soon as you've made contact with the ball.

Either method is okay. Learn to do *one* way with control and confidence. After you've mastered it, then you can try the other.

With either style, here's what you must know about bunting:

- With your left hand at the knob, slide your right hand about twelve inches up toward the barrel (the fat part). Rest the bat (but don't hold it) firmly back between your thumb and second finger.

- If you want to use these fingers again, *don't place them in front of the bat.*

- Stand toward the front of the batter's box (slightly crouched) as you await the pitch.

- *As soon as the pitch is released,* extend your arms enough to get the bat out *in front* of the plate. The earlier you get the bat into position, the more time you have to see the ball and to react to it.

- Your body stays in the box. It is not behind the bat.

- Hold the bat level to the ground. On a pivot bunt, the barrel can be slightly higher than the knob.

- Hold the bat at armpit height. This is the top of the strike zone. If the pitch is higher than the bat, it is out of the strike zone. Let it go.

- Keep your head tucked down, with your eyes looking over the top of the bat.

- Keep your eyes on the ball and watch it all the way.

Bunting Pointers

- The height of the bat is adjusted mostly by the knees. They are the key to a successful bunt. Keep them bent and flexible.

- Meet a low pitch by bending at the knees, not at the waist. Don't reach all the way down with your arms. Lower your body from the knees to bring the bat level toward the ball.

- Aim to bunt the top of the ball with the lower half of the bat. Never raise your bat to meet the ball. You'll pop it up. You want to bunt the ball down to the ground, never up in the air.

- Both hands move the bat. Don't jab at the ball with the barrel.

- The speed of the pitch determines how you contact it. Never push hard or swing at the ball. You don't want to bunt it too hard or too far.

  — A slow pitch should be met with an easy tap of the bat.

  — A fast pitch should be met almost still. Just give it the slightest nudge for direction and let the bat retract upon impact to deaden the ball.

- You don't have to bunt just because you've squared away or pivoted. If the pitch is out of the strike zone, it's okay as long as you don't move the bat toward it. Let it go. Pull the bat back so the umpire won't call it a strike.

- You may have to bunt a bad pitch to protect the runner on a squeeze play at home. If he's come down the line and would be a sure out, you *must* make the bunt (even if it's foul).

- Try to direct your bunt. The best place is near a baseline, away from the pitcher and catcher.

- To beat out a bunt for a hit, the best place is along the third base line.

- Don't watch the ball after you bunt it. Take off for first base and don't look back.

- Don't bunt with two strikes. If you bunt foul, it becomes strike three.

4
Baseball Facts and Folklore

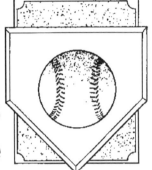

- *The youngest player in history*, Joe Nuxhall, was only 15 years old when he pitched for the Cincinnati Reds in 1944. His debut against the Cardinals was not promising, as he gave up six runs in two thirds of an inning. But Joe was not discouraged. His successful career in the major leagues lasted for 15 more years.

- *The oldest player in history* was Satchel Paige. Nobody knows his exact age. But he was at least 60 years old when he pitched three scoreless innings for the Kansas City A's against Boston in 1965.

  Satchel Paige played most of his career in the Negro National League, and didn't come to the majors until he was over 40 years old. If blacks had been accepted in the majors during his youth, who knows how great he might have been.

Satchel Paige

- *The smallest player in history* was Eddie Gaedel. He was a three-foot seven-inch midget who batted one time for the Cleveland Indians in 1951. He drew a walk.

- *The smallest player in the hall of fame* is "Wee Willie" Keeler. At five feet, four inches, and lacking power, Wee Willie was the greatest place hitter of all time. His motto: "I hit 'em where they ain't."

- *The most unusual lineup in history.* "Uncle" Wilbert Robinson, 1920s Brooklyn Dodgers manager, once handed the umpire a laundry list instead of a lineup before the game.

- *The most amazing comebacks:* The 1991 World Series featured the Twins and the Braves. Both teams had finished in last place the previous year.

Speaking of comebacks, the three greatest comeback teams of all time were

The 1914 Braves

In last place on July fourth, the Braves surged to win their first pennant ever. The "Miracle Braves" went on to sweep the World Series against the A's.

The 1951 Giants

In August they were 13 games behind the Dodgers. With super-rookie Willie Mays, the Giants won all but eight of their last 47 games to tie the race. In the playoffs, the Giants again came from behind to win the pennant on

Bobby Thomson's famous homer. (They lost the World Series to a Yankee team that boasted another super-rookie, Mickey Mantle.)

The 1978 Yankees

In July they were 14 games behind the Red Sox. With pitcher Ron Guidry (25-3) leading the charge, the Yanks' winning streak was highlighted by a September four-game sweep of the Sox. The season ended in a tie. In the playoff, the Yankees again came from behind to win the pennant on Bucky Dent's almost-as-famous homer. (Like Thomson's, Dent's also was a three-run homer with his team trailing by two runs. The final score in both games was 5-4.) The Yankees went on to defeat the Dodgers in the World Series. Bucky Dent was also the Series MVP.

Versatile Players

- Babe Ruth is the only player to pitch in more than 100 games (163) and to get more than 2,000 base hits (2,873).

- Pete Rose is the only one to play more than 600 games, and in an All-Star Game, at each of four different positions (first, second, and third base, and as outfielder). Pete also holds the record for most games played, with 3,562.

- Art Hoelskoetter (Cardinals) played at every position during the 1905–1908 seasons.

- Bert Campaneris (Kansas City A's) played at all nine positions in a single game in 1965.

- Jim Thorpe was the most versatile athlete of all time. He not only played major league baseball (1913–1919), he also won the decathlon and pentathlon track medals in the 1912 Olympics. And from 1919–1926, he enjoyed a Hall of Fame career in the National Football League.

- Riddle: Who is the only person to play for the Brooklyn Dodgers (baseball), the New York Rangers (hockey), and the New York Knicks (basketball)?

  — Answer: Gladys Gooding. She played the organ between innings at Dodger games, and at intermissions for the Rangers and the Knicks.

* * *

- *The most consecutive games* record was held by Lou Gehrig. He played in 2,130 straight games for the 1925–1939 Yankees.

  Cal Ripken, Jr. (Orioles) broke that record late in the 1995 season, with a streak that began in 1982. During the streak, Cal had another equally awesome achievement—he played every single inning for 904 straight games—a total of 8,243 consecutive innings over a five and a half year span. Cal's record is safe for a long time, as the closest contender, Frank Thomas (White Sox) trailed Cal by 1,896 fewer games in 1995.

- The Yankees have won 33 pennants and 22 World Series, beginning in 1921. Their last pennant was won in 1981.

- During the 12 years (1949–1960) of manager Casey Stengel's reign, the Yanks won 10 pennants and seven World Series. They won a record five World Series in a row (1949–1953.)

Jim Thorpe

Casey Stengel

Stengel left after 1960, but the Yanks went on to win four pennants and two World Series in the next four years.

It was the greatest dynasty in the history of any sport. The Yankees failed to win the American League pennant only twice over a 16 year period.

• The flipside of this coin: Chicago Cubs fans have suffered the longest stretch of any team without winning a pennant. The Cubs last won the National League flag in 1945. They have not won a World Series since 1908.

• The longest consecutive winning streak (26 games in a row) is held by the 1916 Giants. They also had a 17-game streak that year. But the rest of the time they were awful. They finished the season in fourth place.

• The longest consecutive game losing streak (23) belongs to the 1961 Phillies.

• The Orioles began 1988 with an 0-21 record, the longest winless streak to start a season.

• A "Triple Crown" winner leads the league in batting average, home runs, and RBIs.

— From 1901 to 1967, the Triple Crown was won 14 times.

— Only two players have won it twice, Rogers Hornsby (Cardinals) in 1922 and 1925, and Ted Williams (Red Sox) in 1942 and 1947.

— No one has won the Triple Crown since 1967.

— The last player to achieve it was Carl Yastrzemski (Red Sox).

— Yaz is the first former Little Leaguer to be inducted into the Hall of Fame.

- Willie Mays (Giants) has played in the most All-Star games. He played in 20 consecutive All-Star games (1954-1973).

Willie Mays

- It's never wise to insult your opponent. Giants manager Bill Terry learned that lesson the hard way.

  In 1934, his arch-rival Brooklyn Dodgers wallowed near the National League cellar. Terry quipped, "Is Brooklyn still in the league?"

  The Giants, tied with the Cardinals for first place, met the Dodgers in the final two games of the season. Brooklyn reminded Terry that they were indeed in the league. They beat the Giants in both games, knocking them out of the race.

5

Throwing
the Ball

These are the basics of throwing. Practice them over and over until it feels natural. After that, you'll do it automatically and you won't have to think about it at all.

How to Hold the Ball

- Put your second and third fingers on top of the ball across the seams.

- These fingers should be slightly apart, and they should not extend over the seam beyond the first knuckle.

- Your thumb is toward the bottom of the ball.

- The inside of your fourth finger holds the right side of the ball.

- Your pinkie hangs loose.

- Don't hold the ball back in the palm of your hand. Hold it firmly with your fingers.

The Throw

Part I (The Windup)

- Shift your body weight back.

- Raise your arm and stretch it back easily at the shoulder. You should feel a slight tension, like stretching a rubber band.

- While your arm moves back, bend your elbow so that your forearm is aimed upward.

- As your hand reaches this point of the windup, point your fingers up at the sky. This cocks your wrist and you are now set to throw.

Part II (The Delivery)

- As you start to throw, point your shoulder at the target.

- Shift your weight forward by taking a step toward the target on your left foot and pushing off your right foot.

- At this point, only the bottom half of your body shifts forward (your chest, shoulders, and arms stay back). Your front hip pulls your weight forward and provides power for the throw.

- As your foot hits the ground (not sooner), your arm begins to come forward. Don't start your arm forward before your foot hits the ground—you'll lose strength and accuracy.

- Now you are into your throw. Extend your arm, keep your elbow up high, and whip your arm forward in a

The Delivery

The Follow-Through

hard, wide overhand arc. Snap your wrist as you let go of the ball.

- Throw with your entire body, not just your arm. Your upper body must now shift forward and follow through along with the arm. As it does, your back foot is pulled around, so that you should be squarely facing the target at the end.

Two final hints:

- Before you throw, get your balance. Your body and the ball should be in your control.

- Try to keep your throw as level as you can. Throw it on a straight line, not on a high arc.

6
World Series Records

(Don't read this if you're a Yankee-hater)

It seems that just about every important World Series record belongs to a Yankee. No wonder! The Yankees have been in 33 World Series, far more than any other team. They have won it 22 times.

The players listed below were all Yankees, unless another team is indicated.

Batting Records

Batting Average (Series): Billy Hatcher (Reds, 1990) —.750

Batting Average (Career): Pepper Martin (Cardinals)—.418

Batting Average (Team): 1960 Yanks—.338 (but they lost the Series to Pittsburgh)

Slugging Average (Series): Lou Gehrig (1928)—1.727

Slugging Average (Career): Reggie Jackson—.755

RBI (Series): Bobby Richardson (1960)—12
RBI (Career): Mickey Mantle—40

Reggie Jackson—"Mr. October"

Runs (Series): Reggie Jackson (1977)—10
     Paul Molitor (Blue Jays, 1993)—10
Runs (Career): Mickey Mantle—42

Hits (Series): Bobby Richardson (1964)—13
  Lou Brock (Cardinals, 1968)—13
  Marty Barrett (Red Sox, 1986)—13
Hits (Career): Yogi Berra—71

Home Runs (Series): Reggie Jackson (1977)—5
Home Runs (Career): Mickey Mantle—18
Home Runs (One Game): Babe Ruth (1926 and 1928)—3
  Reggie Jackson (1977)—3
Home Runs (Consecutive Games): Reggie Jackson
  (1977–78)—4
Home Runs (Series by Team): 1956 Yanks—12
Home Runs (One Game by Team): 1928 Yanks—5

Pitching Records

Whitey Ford holds these Career records: Most Series (11); Games Pitched (22); Games Won (10); Games Lost (8); Strikeouts (94); Consecutive Scoreless Innings (32).

Christy Mathewson (Giants) had the most Career Completed Games (10) and shutouts (4). His three Shutouts in the 1905 Series is an enduring record, as is the entire Giants pitching staff's perfect 0.00 ERA for that Series.

Whitey Ford

Bob Gibson (Cardinals) dominated the 1968 World Series, setting records of 17 strikeouts in one game and 35 in the Series. But it wasn't good enough. The Tigers beat the Cardinals, 4 games to 3.

Stolen Bases

Lou Brock (Cardinals) stole seven bases in 1967 and again in 1968, each a Single Series record. He is tied with Eddie Collins (A's & White Sox) with a Career record of 14.

Most World Series

Yogi Berra's playing career spanned 1947–1963. In those 17 years, he played in 14 World Series and won 10 times. He next managed the Yankees to the 1964 pennant but lost the Series to the Cardinals. Cards manager Johnny Keane replaced Yogi as Yankee skipper in 1965.

7

Playing
the Infield

The most important thing is to *get a good jump on the
ball.* You have a split second to react as soon as the ball is
hit. Be alert, focus your mind on the game situation, and be
ready to spring like a cat.

Jack be nimble, Jack be quick! The "infielder's ready"
position increases your alertness and helps you break swiftly
for the ball. Get into it before every pitch:

- Lean slightly forward at the waist.

- Feet at least shoulder width apart.

- Arms can hang in front, or rest easily (not lean) on your
  knees.

- Body and arms are loose; legs are a bit tensed and ready
  to pounce.

Major league infielders use this stance. You'll not only
play better with it, but you'll really look sharp out there.

Fielding Grounders

The 3 Most Important Points

Get down low. Bend your legs wide apart at the knees and get your body down low to the ground. You can come up for a grounder more easily and quickly than you can go down for it. Get your glove out in front of you, with fingers pointed down and into the dirt, so the ball won't go under it and through your legs.

Keep your eyes on the ball. Watch the ball all the way into the glove. Keep you head down, point your nose at the ball, and never turn your head or look away.

Play the ball; Don't let the ball play you. Move toward every ground ball hit your way. Don't wait for the ball to reach you. Going to the ball lets you play the hop where you choose to, and puts you in control. Waiting for the ball forces you to play the last hop wherever it may go.

When You Field a Grounder

• Try to get your body squarely in front of the ball. You'll get better balance, and you can block the ball if it takes a bad bounce.

• With your feet comfortably apart, step forward with the glove-side foot as you field the ball.

• Catch the ball with both hands. They should be forward of your body (not underneath it) and down low.

• As you scoop the ball, bring it with both hands back up into your gut and get a good grip on it for the throw. (If you must rush your throw, don't waste time with this step.)

• Stay loose and be ready to get a good jump on the ball as soon as it is hit.

Get Down Low, Glove in the Dirt

Get a Good Jump on the Ball

Keep Your Eyes on the Ball All the Way

- Remember that a grounder through the infield often means extra bases and extra runs. Go for it. Dive after it. You've got to knock it down even if you can't field it cleanly to make a play.

- Charge in on slow rollers, and pounce on balls that have stopped rolling. Get your body down really low and keep your eye on the ball. Scoop it up with your bare hand, with your fingers under the ball and your hand turned upward (not down).

Tagging a Runner

Making a Tag at a Base

- *Remember this, and you'll never miss a tag:* The runner must touch the base. The base is on the ground. He can only touch it with his foot or his hand on the ground. If he has no place to touch it on the ground, he will be out.

- Therefore, *always tag low at the base.* Here's how:
  — Make sure you catch the ball thrown to you.
  — Straddle the front of the base (the side facing the runner). One foot (at the instep) should be beside each of the front corners of the base.
  — Hold the glove (with the ball) down low in the dirt directly in front of the base. As the runner's foot or hand comes to the base, move the glove slightly left or right as needed to make the tag. Keep the glove down.
  — As you can see, this way you have given the runner no place to touch the base safely. He can't touch the sides of the base because your legs block the sides. And you have taken away the front of the base with your glove.

Tag Low, Give Him No Place to Go

— Never reach out to the runner, or you will lose this advantage. Let the runner slide into your waiting glove.

• When making a tag:

— Bend your knees.

— Get your body low to the ground.

— Keep your arms loose (not stiff).

— Hold the ball tightly in your glove.

— Tag with the back of the glove. You don't have to touch the runner with the ball itself, only with the glove holding the ball.

— Pull the glove up and away as soon as the tag is made.

— Be careful not to drop the ball or to have it kicked out of your glove.

73

Tagging a Runner off the Base

• A runner between the bases will be trying to evade you (unlike a runner tagged at a base). His upper body presents you with the biggest target. You should aim to tag him between the waist and shoulders if you can.

• Be alert and stay loose. Let the runner make the first definite move, so you don't commit yourself too early or get faked out of position.

• Hold the ball tightly when you make the tag to prevent it from being knocked loose.

"Second Tags"

• A runner sometimes will step off a base just after he's reached it safely. Try a "second tag." Turn away from him, as though your attention is elsewhere. (Perhaps fake tossing the ball back to the pitcher.) Then suddenly reach back and tag him with the ball. You might just catch him napping.

Infielder Throws

• Before you throw, get your balance. Your body and the ball should be in your control. Concentrate on your target as you make the throw.

• Sometimes you may have to throw on the run and you won't have time to get set. Practice these throws so you'll be ready.

• Never throw the ball if there is no chance to get the out. The more the ball is thrown, the more chance for disaster. Make smart throws. Don't throw unnecessarily.

- Before you throw to your teammate, be sure he is looking at you and that he's expecting the ball.

- Cut back on the power of your throw if your teammate is close to you, or if be lacks the ability to catch a hard throw.

Pop Flies

- Call for all pop-ups, LOUD AND CLEAR.
  - — Be sure you can make the catch before you call for it.
  - — Don't call for the ball until it has started to come down.
  - — If another player has called for it, get out of his way, (but back him up).

- Catch the ball with two hands.

- On a pop-up foul near the fence, take a quick look at the ball. Then go fast and directly (with your arm extended) to the fence. Once you've located the fence, you can look back up and concentrate on catching the ball.

- On a pop-up into the sun:
  - — Don't stare into the sun.
  - — Shield your eyes with your glove.
  - — Look quickly at the ball as it goes into the sun, then look

away, and then look up again. The ball might now be below the sun where you can see it.

— If all else fails:

DUCK

PRAY

Double Plays on Grounders

There aren't many grounder double plays in kids' baseball. That makes it more fun when you get one.
Here's how:

- *Get one out for sure.* Double plays are flashy, but concentrate on getting the first out before going for the DP.

- Toss the ball to the pivot man above the waist. Let him see the ball in your hand. If it's a short toss, underhand it directly. (Don't loop it.)

- The pivot man should catch the ball with two hands. This lets him get it out of his glove easily for the next throw.

- Pivot man: Make sure you touch the base *while you have the ball*—not before you receive it or after you've thrown it to first.

Rundowns

Trapping a runner between bases is probably the most exciting play in kids' baseball. It's also a lot of fun.
But a rundown can be a real bummer if you don't do it right. Here's what you must know:

- *Make as few throws as possible.* The best rundowns have only one (sometimes zero) throws. The more you throw the ball, the more chance of a poor throw, an error, or the runner finding a way to escape.

- Get the ball into the hands of the fielder who is in front of the runner. Always try to chase the runner *back* toward the previous base. Then if you don't get him out, at least he won't have advanced a base.

- Run hard at the runner, at full speed. Don't hesitate—this is a chase!

- Try to get the runner to break toward a base and commit himself so that it's difficult for him to reverse direction.

- Hold the ball high, ready to throw as you run. If the runner has not yet committed, do *one* (not more) arm fake.

- At that moment, if he hesitates continue to run at him and make the tag. If he breaks to the other base, throw immediately to get him out. (Don't hold the ball too long. Make a firm throw. Don't lob it or it may arrive too late.)

- The fielder receiving the throw should stand near the base, not up the basepath. This cuts the runner's chance to speed past him as he awaits the throw.

- Fielders in a rundown should not stand directly on the basepath. Instead, they should position themselves slightly inside of it. This has two advantages. First, you can throw on the side of the runner and not over his head. Second, if you block the runner without the ball in your hand, the runner is automatically safe ("obstruction").

- All infielders should take part in the rundown, and be ready to take a throw or back up a ball that gets away. On a rundown between third and home, the pitcher should back up the catcher at the plate.

- Never forget that there may be other runners on the bases. Be especially aware of runners on bases ahead of the rundown.

Other Infield Pointers

- Never assume an easy out. When you make a play, don't relax. Make it snappy.

- On steals of second base, the shortstop and second baseman should decide before the game who will take the throw. (Usually it's the shortstop.) The other player must back him up, at least 10 feet behind the base.

- When taking the throw on a steal (or any other play), first be sure to catch the ball. Don't start to make the tag until you've got control of the ball.

- Watch for the runner to touch each base. If he missed a base, you can appeal to the umpire to call him out.

- As soon as you've made a catch, look to see what the runners are doing. (Are they tagging up? Can you double them off?) There may still be another play you can make.

- If you make an error, don't get rattled. The play is not over. Get to the ball and look around to see if you can catch a runner at another base.

- If you have a choice, always make the play unassisted. Don't throw the ball if you don't have to.

- On a grounder with a runner on third (and less than two out), you can either look at him, make him hesitate, and then throw quickly to first base, or fake a throw to first and see if the runner breaks for home.

- When receiving a throw on a force at second or third, stretch for the ball like a first baseman.

Two Rules You Should Know

Interference
The infielder has the right of way when fielding a *batted* ball. Don't worry about the runner. He will be out if he interferes with you.

Obstruction
The runner has the right of way on a *thrown* ball. The infielder cannot obstruct the runner on the basepaths while waiting for the throw (or otherwise). He can only obstruct if he actually has the ball in his possession.

Runner Interference

Playing First Base

- When you take a throw, the first rule is: *catch the ball!* Nothing else matters. It does no good for you to have your foot on the base if you don't have the ball. If the throw gets past you, it means extra bases. So always be sure you *catch the ball!*

- On a ball to the infield (other than one hit at you):

  — Get to first base immediately.

— Stand with the back part of both feet against the inside of the bag. Don't stand on top of the base. Stay loose!

— Wait to see where the throw is going before you make your move to catch it.

— On a good throw, step out toward it, and put the ball of your foot against the bag. Stretch your glove out to meet it. Watch the flight of the ball all the way into your mitt.

— On close plays, stretch way out. But remember that the greater the stretch, the lower your body is to the ground. You aren't in as good a position to catch a high throw. You may have to give up some stretch in order to make the catch.

• Always expect a poor throw and be ready to move for it.

— The second you realize the throw will pull you off the bag, don't waste precious time. *Get off the bag right away* and go to catch the ball.

— If it's so wild you can't catch it, leave the base. Run immediately to where the ball is heading and throw it back into play.

— If a poor throw pulls you off the bag, see if you can tag the runner before he reaches first base.

• On a throw into the dirt in front of you:

— If you can stretch and catch it before it hits the ground, do so.

— If it's too far in front of you, don't stretch. Instead, stand and back up toward the base and catch it on the big bounce. Use two hands.

On a Close Play, Stretch Way Out

— If it will hit the dirt close to you, get your mitt down as close to the ball as you can. Don't swipe at the ball. Try to let it bounce into your glove.

— In any case, you must do two things:

1. Keep your eyes on the ball all the way. Don't look away.

2. Block the ball with your body if you don't catch it.

• If the batter hits a single, watch him after he crosses first base. If he turns toward second, or if he overruns first and makes any move toward second, try to tag him out before he returns to first base.

Fielding Your Position

A first baseman's normal position is about six feet over toward second and about eight feet deep. With a weak hitter or a force at another base, play in closer to the infield grass.

Grounders

— Field any ground ball you can reach.

— Always make the play unassisted if you can win the race. If the pitcher is covering first base, wave him away so you don't have a collision. (Wave with the hand that is *not* holding the ball.)

— If you can't win the race yourself, toss the ball to the pitcher who should be covering the bag.

The Toss to the Pitcher Covering First

— Toss it underhand, medium hard.

— Toss it on a direct line. Don't loop it high.

— Toss it in front of the pitcher as he heads for first. Lead the pitcher with the toss.

— Try to get the ball to him before he reaches the base.

Playing the Bunt

My suggestion is to stay at your base and let the pitcher and catcher field all bunts. On a hard bunt past the pitcher, let the second baseman field it.

Some coaches will disagree. Ask your coach to set the strategy here.

What Kind of Glove to Use

• The best choice is a "first baseman's mitt." This is designed specifically for the position, and it will give you a big advantage.

• A first baseman's mitt cannot be used at any other position.

• Ask your league if they can make a first baseman's mitt available to everyone. It can be expensive for you to go out and buy one, especially if you don't play first base all the time.

• Otherwise, you should play first base with a regular large fielder's glove with a big pocket and web. Break it in so that it becomes soft and flexible.

Playing Second Base

• Second base is called "The Keystone Sack" because infield play centers around second. It's where the action is.

• A second baseman must be quick on his feet and aware of the fine points of the game. He must:

— Back up throws to the shortstop on steals of second (stand about 10 feet back, near the outfield grass).

— Be ready to take the force throw at second with a runner on first.

— Cover second base on a ball hit to left field.

— Be the cutoff man on a ball hit to the right side of the outfield.

— Catch pop flies that are too deep for the first base-man to handle.

— Check with your coach for strategy on playing bunts. (See comment on this in the First Base section.)

- Above all, there are two things a second baseman must always do:

1. BE ALERT!
2. HUSTLE!

- A second baseman's normal position is about halfway between first and second. With no one on base, or a strong hitter, he should play deep. With runners, play closer in. With a particularly weak hitter, play in at the grass, to be able to field a slow grounder more quickly.

Call for the Cutoff

Playing Shortstop

- The shortstop is the sparkplug of the infield and the glue that holds it together. You can energize it with peppy play and chatter.

— Hustle in the field. Run to your position. Keep your head high. Move the ball briskly.

— Don't be quiet. Keep "talking it up." Encourage your teammates—your enthusiasm will be contagious.

— Keep the other infielders aware of the game situation. Tell them how many outs; if there's a force; where to throw; etc.

— You must be the leader, and you can fire up your team to go all out and win.

- A shortstop must:
  - Take the throw on a steal of second.
  - With a runner on base, back up the pitcher when the catcher returns the pitch to him (in case the ball gets away).
  - Be ready to take the force throw at second with a runner on first.
  - Cover second base on a ball hit to right field.
  - Be the cutoff man on a ball hit to the left side of the outfield.
  - Catch pop flies that are too deep for the third baseman to handle.

- A shortstop's normal position is deep and over toward second base. More hits go "over the middle" than "through the hole" (between short and third). With luck, your third baseman can cover some of the hits in the hole.

Playing Third Base

- Third base is called "The Hot Corner." You stand closer to the plate than any other baseman. Balls come at you off the bat like bullets.

- To play third base, you must be:
  1. READY AND SWIFT
  2. CONFIDENT AND FEARLESS

- A third baseman must:
  - On hard grounders and line drives, brace yourself, stand your ground, challenge the ball and grab it. If

you can't make the play cleanly, knock it down, dive for it, or do whatever you must, but *don't let the ball get past you.*

You've Got to Be Quick and Tough

— On slow rollers and stopped balls, charge in and make the play.

— Cut off all grounders you can reach. Don't let the ball go to the shortstop if you can field it. (Exception: If there's a play to be made at third, you might stay at your base if the shortstop can field the ball.)

— In bunt situations, play up close and charge the ball. (Exception: If there's a runner on second, you might stay at your base and let the pitcher or catcher field the ball.)

• Special Pointers for Third Basemen:

— With bases loaded and less than two out: On a grounder to third, don't step on the base. Throw to the catcher for the force at home.

— With a runner on second or third, be ready for a play. Go back to the bag after every pitch.

— In general, never leave third base uncovered if there is a runner on first or second.

- A third baseman's normal position is at least six feet off the foul line and about five feet deep from the bag. Most kids swing late, and the average hitter is not likely to pull a fast pitch down the line. (With a slow pitcher or a lefty batter, play closer to the line.)

Infield Bloopers

"Piano Legs" Hickman (Giants third baseman) set a record for the most errors in a season (87) back in 1900.

His record didn't last long. The very next year, Bill Keister (Orioles shortstop) muffed 97 chances. Keister's record still stands.

There is a good reason for all those errors. Have you ever seen a 1900 baseball glove? It was half the size of today's glove. The fingers were short and the pocket was almost nonexistent.

The 1912 World Series

The Giants took a 2-1 lead over the Red Sox in the top of the tenth inning of the final game. Then their fielding fell apart in the bottom of the inning.

The lead-off hitter lofted a soft fly ball which landed in and then fell out of the glove of center fielder Fred Snodgrass. Superstar pitcher Christy Mathewson walked the next batter.

Hall of Famer Tris Speaker came up and hit an easy foul pop-up off the first base line. Mathewson and the catcher and first baseman waited together under the ball. *Nobody called for it.* Nobody caught it. Speaker took advantage of his new life and singled in the tying run. The winning run followed. The Giants blew the Series on blunders that would have embarrassed a Little League team.

Tris Speaker

The 1986 World Series

Have you heard of "the Curse of the Babe?" You have if you're a Red Sox rooter. Your team has not won a World Series since they traded Babe Ruth to the Yankees in 1920.

In the 1986 Series, it appeared that the Curse was about to end. The Sox led 3-2 in games, and 5-3 in the bottom of the tenth of Game six. With two out, they were one pitch away from victory. The Mets put together three singles to make it 5-4.

The next batter, Mookie Wilson, watched a wild pitch sail past him, scoring the tying run from third. Mookie then topped an easy dribbler to Sox first baseman Bill Buckner. It should have been the third out. But Buckner *didn't get his glove down into the dirt.* The ball rolled slowly under his glove and through his legs as the winning run crossed the plate.

The Series was tied at 3-3. The Mets won Game seven. The "Curse of the Babe" lives on.

8

Playing
the Outfield

Okay, so your coach stuck you in the outfield and you're not exactly thrilled.

Cheer up! You'll have fun if you just remember three things.

1. YOU ARE NOT IN "NEVER NEVER LAND". Center field is not Siberia. You may be farther from the action, but you are still on the ballfield where *things happen*!

— Don't daydream. Keep your mind involved in every play. Be aware of what's happening on every pitch.

— Don't count the dandelions or watch the butterflies.

— Be alert and ready to spring into action.

— Back up infield throws and grounders. They may find their way into the outfield.

— Back up other outfielders.

— Get a good jump on balls hit your way.

— Know where you'll throw the ball when you get it.

2. YOU ARE VERY IMPORTANT! A good play in the outfield can save several runs. An infield error usually costs only one run, but an outfield error can be a disaster.

3. YOU CAN DO IT!

- *Have confidence!* You can catch those high flies and make the long throw.
- *Take pride in yourself!* Practice. Practice until you get it right.

An outfielder's *second* most importance job is to catch the ball. Your *most* important job is to block the ball and not let it roll by.

Certainly, make the catch when you can. But whatever you do, don't let the ball get past you. If you can't catch it or block it, *hustle* after it.

Never hold onto the ball for more than a second or two. As long as it is in the outfield, the runners will fly around the bases. Get rid of it fast.

Return the ball immediately to the infield. If there's a cutoff man, throw it to him. If you're not sure, throw it to *any* infielder. Hurry it back to where it will do some good.

How to Catch a Fly Ball

- Watch the ball as it comes off the bat. *Keep your eyes on the ball all the way.* (Exception: If it's hit into the sun. See the Pop Flies section in Chapter 7.)

- Get moving right away in the general direction of the fly. Try to judge where the ball is heading.

    — If you have time, run to a spot just slightly behind where you expect it to drop. Get there quickly, ahead of the ball, and wait for it.

- Line the ball up with your nose. Catch it in front of you. Don't stand to the side of it.

Catch it High and out in Front

- You'll catch most flies higher than your waist. Your glove's fingers should point up. (If the ball is below your waist, point your glove fingers downward.)

- Put the glove up toward the ball and *catch it as high as you can.*

  — Use two hands for the catch. Your bare hand will keep the ball from popping out of the glove.

  — Try to catch it in the webbing of the glove.

- Above all, *concentrate on making the catch.* Focus your mind on holding onto the ball as it hits your glove.

Going Back for a Deep Fly

Think football! How does a wide receiver sprint after a long forward pass? He doesn't backpedal.

— He runs sideways with crossover steps.

— His weight is forward.

— He pushes off on the balls of his feet.

— His shoulders are pointed toward the ball.

— His mind is totally concentrated on making the catch.

Be like Jerry Rice!

— Don't backpedal.

— Turn your body toward the fly and take a step in that direction.

— Cross over with the other leg, and run in a crossover stride.

— Don't run with the glove reaching out. Put your glove up toward the ball only as you are about to catch it.

Fielding a Grounder

- On a single with no other baserunners, you don't need to rush your throw. You can kneel on your left knee to field the grounder.

- Field all other grounders just like an infielder. Charge in at the ball; get down low and square to the ball.

- Make sure to *block the ball*. Don't let it get past you.

Throwing to the Infield

- After the catch, take a "crow hop" toward your target. (A crow hop is a little hop forward on your right foot as you start your throw. It gives you momentum and puts more power into the throw.)

- Throw overhand.

- Don't throw the ball in a high arc. Throw it on a direct line.

- Try to hit the cutoff man. If there's no cutoff, throw ahead of the lead runner.

- Return the ball to the infield *immediately.*

Other Outfield Pointers

- Play most batters shallow rather than deep. There are a lot more short bloopers than deep flies in kids' baseball, even by the best hitters. But be ready to hightail it back to the fence in case you guessed wrong.

- Call for all fly balls if another fielder is near. (Read about this in the Pop Flies section of Chapter 7.)

- Many outfields contain holes, dips, mounds, rocks, sticks, and other unpleasant surprises. Check your territory before the game. A sprained ankle (or worse) will ruin your season.

- Never throw your glove or your hat at a ball. Never catch a ball in your hat. (It's a three base penalty.)

- Don't catch that *foul* fly ball *if* the winning run is at third base and *if* there are less than two out. You don't want the runner to tag up and score.

- Hey, right fielder—Wake Up! On a sharp single to right, you might still be able to throw out a slow batter at first base. Or if he makes a wide turn, you might throw behind him and catch him before he returns to first.

Outfield Gems

You may have seen Willie Mays' (Giants) 1954 World Series catch on TV. From shallow center field, Willie raced all the way to the bleachers under Vic Wertz's (Indians) towering blast. Running with his back to the plate, he reached out to haul it in over his shoulder. Then in one motion, Willie whirled and hurled the ball back to the infield, preventing the runners from scoring.

Equally awesome (though not as famous) is Al Gionfriddo's (Dodgers) 1947 World Series catch. Gionfriddo, racing across the left field grass at Yankee Stadium, leaped to snatch Joe Di Maggio's home run drive before it went over the bullpen fence.

The most amazing outfield catch happened in the 1912 World Series. Harry Hooper (Red Sox) robbed Larry Doyle (Giants) of a homer, with a bare-handed catch as the ball was about to go into the stands.

There was the time (Cardinal) Frenchy Bordagaray's cap blew off as he chased a ball in the outfield. Frenchy stopped, turned around, and went to get his cap. Then he ran after the ball. (You wouldn't do that, would you?)

9

The Pitcher

The pitcher is the team's centerpiece. He stands in the center of the diamond, and his team's fate revolves around him. If he's "on," they'll probably win, and vice versa. If he loses his control, forget about it. His eight teammates are helpless if he can't find the plate.

Control is the key to good pitching. Work on your control, and your speed will increase as you gain confidence in your ability to throw strikes.

Some Pitching Pointers

• Make your first pitch a strike. Get ahead of the hitter right away. It puts the pressure on him and takes it off you. Get a second strike and then he'll have to protect the plate! He may swing at the next pitch out of the strike zone.

• Stronger hitters: Throw at different speeds and at different areas of the strike zone. Pitch them mostly low and outside. You'll be pitching away from their power.

- Weaker hitters: Don't let up. Don't walk them. You don't want to lose an easy out.
  - Don't throw change-ups to them. They may prefer the slower speed.

- *Never lose your cool.* Things will go wrong. Your fielder (or you) may make an error; you'll throw some bad pitches; the ump will blow a call against you. It's part of the game. *You must shrug it off.*
  - Mutter a few naughty words (under your breath).
  - Kick the dirt (one time).
  - Allow yourself 10 seconds of misery.
  - Then, *forget it and think ahead.* Pull yourself together and play the game. You can't control your pitches unless you control yourself.

- Take your time between pitches.
  - Don't rush.
  - Take a deep breath.
  - Get your balance.
  - Collect your thoughts.
  - Focus on your target (the mitt).
  - Throw a strike!

- Don't be afraid to throw the ball over the plate. Don't throw outside for fear of hitting the batter. (You probably won't.)

- Don't hold back. Throw hard. Let 'er rip! Some kids restrain themselves and throw only from the elbow. You lose control. The ball will bounce in front of the plate. Have confidence. Throw with your whole arm and follow through.

- Don't steer the ball. Be like a shortstop throwing to first base. Fix on your target (the mitt), and don't think about it, just throw It.

- Make your "pitchout" high and outside, so the catcher will be in position to throw right away. Be sure you have a good signal and that the catcher is expecting it.

- Pitch high in the strike zone if you expect a bunt. A high pitch is more likely to be bunted up in the air.

Protecting Your Arm

- Warm up and stretch out before you pitch. Start with soft lobs, and gradually throw harder. Throw only ten or fifteen pitches at full speed.

- Don't overdo practicing at another position before the game. If you tire your arm practicing the long throw from shortstop, you won't be in condition to pitch.

- *If your arm hurts, stop pitching.* Tell your coach and your parents.

- Don't practice pitching every day. Skip at least one day and give your arm a rest.

- *Don't throw curveballs.* I know it's macho and it's hard to resist, but don't do it. Your body is still developing. (Give it a few more years.) You can seriously hurt your arm, shoulder, and elbow. It's not worth it.

- Keep your arm warm at all times. In cool weather, wear a jacket before the game and between innings.

Fielding Your Position

- The moment you release your pitch, you become a fielder.

- — Be alert. Get to the ball quickly. Pounce on it.
- — Block any hard hit you can get your glove on. If you don't, it will go up the middle, and into center field.
- — Step off the mound before you throw to a base. You'll have better balance and control.

- On a wild pitch or passed ball:
  - — Help the catcher locate the ball. Shout to him. Tell him where to find it.
  - — With a runner on third, dash in and cover home right away. Hold the ball firmly when you make the tag.

- On a pop-up (fair or foul) with a runner on third, the runner can tag up.
  - — Cover home if the catcher is making the catch.
  - — Back up the catcher if an infielder is catching it.

- Back up the catcher or third baseman on throws from the outfield.

- Get involved in any rundown. Back up the catcher, the third baseman, or the first baseman, depending on the situation.

Covering First Base

- On *every* grounder to your left of the mound, run immediately toward first base to take the throw. Except:
  - — Field it yourself if you can.
  - — Field all bunts the catcher can't handle.

- When covering first base:
  - — Don't run directly toward first base. Run toward the baseline about 10 feet before the base.

— Before you reach the line, veer over toward the base. Don't run in the baseline.

— Look to see where the base is. Then take your eye off the base and watch for the ball. Concentrate on catching the ball.

— If everything goes exactly right, the first baseman will lead you with his toss. He'll toss the ball in front of you before you reach the base.

— Have you heard of Murphy's Law? Things usually don't go exactly right. Expect the toss to be anywhere.

— Above all, *don't overrun the toss. Keep the ball in front of you.* Slow down a bit until you see the ball. You can't reach back if the ball is thrown behind you.

— Try to touch the inside of first base with your right foot. Then push off and turn toward the infield, to avoid a collision with the runner.

The Pitch

This section tells you how to pitch. It is only a guide. You don't have to follow it exactly. Adjust to find the style that is right for you. But remember, these *are* the basics. Stick to them as closely as you comfortably can.

Develop your own motion. Then practice it until it becomes natural and you no longer have to think about it.

Find your groove. Use the same motion over and over. Consistency will give you *control.*

The Grip

The fast ball: Grip the ball across the seams with your second and third fingers. Leave a little space between the ball and the palm of your hand. Don't grip it too tightly.

Change-ups: Hold the ball back against the palm of your hand. The grip changes the speed. Throw with the same motion as the fast ball, but release it with a firm wrist (don't snap your wrist as you would a fast ball).

— Use the change-up as a strategy.

— Throw it only when you're ahead in the count, particularly with two strikes on the batter.

The Fast Ball Grip

The Change-Up Grip

The Full Windup

This description is for right-handed pitchers. If you are a southpaw, read "right" to be "left" and vice versa.

Before the Windup:

- Relax. Don't rush. Get your body and mind ready.
- The ball is in the pocket of your glove.
- Look at the target. Pitch to the mitt. Concentrate on it. Forget all about the batter and the runners. Keep your eyes on the target from the start through the finish of the pitch.

The Windup

- Start with both feet on the rubber, facing the plate.
- Take a short step back with your left foot and shift your weight onto it. Rock your arms back loosely at the same time.
- Lift your right foot and place the outside of it (sideways) along the front of the rubber. Find a comfortable spot. (Your body will begin to turn toward the third base line.)
- As your foot goes to the rubber, rock your hands forward and up, and bring them together above your head.
- *As part of the same motion:*
  - Raise your left leg straight up. Your knee is bent, and at about belt high.
  - Pivot your body by rotating your hips and shoulders so they point at the plate (or slightly past it).
- Then, keeping both hands together, slowly lower them to your chest.

- Find a point at which you have good balance, and *hold still* there like a statue, for a second.
- Fix the target in your mind, and prepare to push off the rubber and throw.

The Stride

- Shift your weight back. Your right leg bends slightly.
- Swing your right arm downward like a pendulum and reach all the way back toward center field. Keep your hand on top of the ball.
- As your arm goes back, begin your stride by opening your left shoulder and chest toward the plate. This puts spring into your body and power into your pitch.
- Drive hard off the rubber with your right leg. Feel your lower body shift forward. *Keep your arm and upper body back.*
- Stride toward the plate with your left leg.
- Stride comfortably forward; don't overstride. Land on the ball of your foot, left knee bent, toes pointing at the plate.

The Delivery

- You have not yet begun to throw the ball.
- As your striding foot hits the ground, your right arm begins its upward arc. Your upper body is still leaning back.
- Feel yourself wound up and about to uncoil like a spring as you go into your pitch.

- Keep your arm reaching back behind your body in a wide overhand arc. As it approaches shoulder height it will bend at the elbow in an "L" shape, pointing upward.

- Keep your elbow above shoulder height as you bring your arm forward.

- *Think of your arm as a whip which your body hurls into the pitch.*

- *Everything stays back.* Each part of your motion is led forward by the part in front of it.

  — Your stride pulls (leads) your upper back and right shoulder. They provide the power.

  — Your right shoulder pulls (leads) your upper arm and elbow.

  — Your upper arm and elbow pull (lead) your forearm.

  — Your forearm pulls (leads) your wrist.

  — Your wrist is bent back and ready to throw.

- At the top of your arc:

  — Pull down on the ball with your fingers.

  — Snap your wrist.

  — Let it fly!

The Follow-Through

You must finish with a strong follow-through. Without it, you lose power and control.

- *Your target is the mitt.* Focus only on it, not on the batter. Try to throw the ball **through** the mitt, not just to it.

- Don't hold back. Fire the ball like a cannon shot. Intensify your maximum effort into the *last moment* of the pitch.

- Let the momentum of your arm and shoulder carry your body into the follow-through.

- Your right arm continues across your body, and your hand finishes down outside your left knee.

- Your right leg swings around. Land on the ball of your right foot, about even with the left foot. Both feet point at the plate.

- End up in ready position to field the ball! Face the plate squarely, with the glove in front of your body.

Omissions

I have purposely left a few subjects out of this chapter.

Balks: Although Little League play includes balks, many local leagues don't enforce this rule. It's a technicality better explained directly by the coach, when it applies.

Holding the runner at first base: In most youth leagues, you are not permitted to leave a base until the pitch crosses the plate.

The set position: Because there is no leading off a base, most pitchers use the full windup. If you prefer the "set position," the basics are pretty much the same after you begin your stride.

The Greatest Pitching Feats of All Time

1917—Fred Toney (Reds) and Hippo Vaughn (Cubs) pitched the only nine-inning double no-hitter in history. Jim Thorpe drove in the winning run in the 10th inning to give the Reds a 1-0 win.

1920—The longest game ever played went 26 innings. It was called for darkness with the score tied 1-1. The starters (Leon Cadore—Dodgers, and Joe Oeschger—Braves) each pitched the entire 26 innings.

1934—In the All-Star game, Carl Hubbell (Giants) struck out five (in a row) of the greatest sluggers of all time. They were Hall of Famers Babe Ruth, Lou Gehrig, Jimmie Foxx, Al Simmons, and Joe Cronin.

Fernando Valenzuela (Dodgers) matched this feat in the 1986 game by whiffing Don Mattingly, Cal Ripken, Jr., Jesse Barfield, Lou Whittaker, and Ted Higuera.

1938—Johnny VanderMeer (Reds) pitched back-to-back no hitters against the Braves and the Dodgers.

1947—Ewell Blackwell (Reds) nearly did the exact same thing in the same month against the same teams. He no-hit the Braves, and he just missed a no-hitter in the ninth inning against the Dodgers. As Yogi Berra would say, it was "déjà vu all over again."

1952—It was the greatest game ever pitched in professional baseball. 19-year-old Ron Necciai of the Class D Appalachian League Bristol (VA) Twins faced just 27 batters and struck out every single one of them. That's about as perfect as you can get.

1956—Don Larsen (Yankees) beat the Dodgers in the only perfect World Series game ever. The last out was a called third strike on Dale Mitchell, who at the time had the lowest strikeout percentage of all active National Leaguers.

1959—Harvey Haddix (Pirates) pitched 12 perfect innings of a scoreless tie against the Braves. He gave up his first hit in the 13th inning and lost the game, 1-0.

1970—Tom Seaver (Mets) fanned 10 San Diego Padres in a row. He struck out 19 in the game.

1986—Roger Clemens (Red Sox) threw 20 strikeouts in a 3-1 win over the Seattle Mariners.

1986—Jim Deshaies (Astros) struck out the first eight Dodger batters to come up, in pitching the first complete game of his career.

1988—Dennis Eckersley, A's reliever, saved all four games of the American League Championship Series against the Red Sox.

Roger Clemens—20 K's

Important Pitching Records

Wins:

- *Most Wins In a Season:* Jack Chesbro (Yankees) won 41 games in 1904. But his wild pitch on the last day of the season (a spitball) cost the Yanks the pennant.

- *Most Consecutive Wins:* Carl Hubbell (Giants) won 24 straight games over the 1936–37 seasons.

- *Highest Career Winning Percentage:* Whitey Ford (Yankees) won 236 games and lost 106 for a .690 career record.

- *Most Career Wins:* Cy Young (Red Sox) won 511 games. He was nicknamed 'Cy' because his pitch was like a cyclone that blew batters away.

  — The Cy Young Award goes to the best pitcher in each league. Only Steve Carlton (Phillies) has won it four times. Only Greg Maddux (Braves) has won it in three consecutive years. As we go to press (1995), it looks like he'll make it four in a row.

Shutouts

- *Most Shutouts In a Season:* Grover Cleveland Alexander (Phillies) pitched 16 shutouts in 1916.

- *Most Career Shutouts:* Walter Johnson (Washington Senators) had 110 shutouts.

- *Most Consecutive Shutout Innings:* Orel Hershiser (Dodgers)—59 in 1988.

- *Most Consecutive Shutout Games:* Don Drysdale (Dodgers)—six in 1968.

Earned Run Average

- *Lowest ERA in a Season:* Dutch Leonard (Red Sox)—1.01 in 1914.

- *Lowest Career ERA:* Ed Walsh (White Sox)—1.82.

Strikeouts

- *Most Strikeouts in a Game:* Roger Clemens' (Red Sox) 20 strikeouts (1986) was the most in nine innings. Tom Cheney (Washington Senators) actually struck out 21 (1962), but in a 16-inning game.

- *Most Strikeouts in a Season:* Nolan Ryan (Angels)—383 in 1973.

- *Most Career Strikeouts:* Nolan Ryan—5,714.

- *Most Career Strikeouts Per Nine Innings:* Nolan Ryan averaged 9.54 strikeouts for every nine innings he pitched. That's better than one strikeout in every inning.

No-Hitters

- *Most Career No-Hitters:* Nolan Ryan pitched seven no-hitters. This is probably the most stupendous pitching feat of all. Consider this: In second place is Sandy Koufax (Dodgers) with just four no-hitters; Bob Feller (Indians) is third with three. No other pitcher in history has thrown more than two no-hitters.

Best Record with a Losing Team

- This feat is almost as awesome. Steve Carlton won 15 straight games and 27 for the season, for the last place 1972 Phillies. The team was dreadful, winning only 59 games altogether.

Nolan Ryan—There Were 4 More Yet to Come

Interesting Pitching Facts

✓ Which pitchers have *lost* the most games in this century?
They are three of the greatest:

115

Cy Young—316 losses (he won 511).

Nolan Ryan—292 losses (he won 324).

Walter Johnson—279 losses (he won 416).

✓ Babe Ruth (Yankees) hit his 60th home run in 1927 off Tom Zachary (Washington Senators). They became teammates in 1928 when Zachary was traded to the Yankees. Tom posted a 12-0 record for them in 1929.

✓ Babe Ruth was a great pitcher for the Boston Red Sox before he became a Yankee slugger. In 1917, Ruth walked the first batter and was ejected from the game for arguing with the umpire. Ernie Shore came in to relieve the Babe. The runner was then thrown out stealing second base. Shore retired every batter after that and pitched a perfect game in relief.

✓ Dizzy and Paul Dean (Cardinals) were one of the great brother pitching combinations. Before the 1934 season, Dizzy boasted, "Me and Paul will win 45 games between us." Poor grammar, but he made good on his promise. Dizzy won 30 and Paul won 19. Then in the World Series against the Tigers, Dizzy and Paul won two games apiece and each had an ERA of less than 2.00. Dizzy was voted that year's National League MVP.

✓ Hall of Famer Bob Feller (Indians) entered the majors (1936) when he was only 17 years old. He struck out 15 batters in his first game, and 17 a few weeks later. Then he returned home to finish high school before continuing his baseball career. Feller is the youngest ever to pitch and win a complete game.

Bob Feller—Schoolboy Star

✓ Virgil Trucks (Tigers) pitched two no-hitters in 1952. He won only three other games, and had a 5-19 record.

* * *

✓ *Why is a lefty called a "southpaw?"* It's because the sun sets in the west! All major league diamonds are designed so that the batter faces east. (Imagine having to hit a fast

117

curve with the sun in your eyes). The pitcher stands on the mound facing west. Can you figure out what makes a lefty a "southpaw?"

✓ *Why does the pitcher raise one leg when he goes into his windup?* Because if he raised them both, he'd fall down.

10

The Catcher

A Catcher has to be *smart,* and he has to be *tough.*

- A good catcher is the field general. He takes charge of his team. He controls his pitcher. He can position his fielders. He should remind his infield of the game situation (how many out, force play, etc.).

- A good catcher expects plenty of bumps and bruises. There will be foul tips, wild pitches, crashing runners. There will be some pain.

- A good catcher was born to catch. He loves his position. It's where the action is. It's the most difficult position in baseball. It is also the most satisfying and the most fun.

The Crouch (Taking the Pitch)

- Your crouch should be *comfortable;* your body *flexible.*

- A crouch is not a squat. Raise your butt up from the ground, slightly higher than your knees. Your heels touch the ground—but get your weight toward the balls of your feet. Don't tense up. Find yourself a stance that lets you feel at ease.

- Hold your mitt out toward the pitcher. Don't keep it in by your chest.

- Some catchers leave their index (second) finger outside the back of the mitt. If it feels good to you, it's okay.

The Crouch

- Don't stay too far back. Get close to the batter, but be sure you're out of reach of the swinging bat.

- Hold your bare hand behind the mitt for protection (not behind your back). Keep it in a loose fist with the thumb inside.

- Get your body set *before* the pitcher begins his windup. Give him a good target with your mitt. *Don't move your body or your target* once he starts his motion.

- Extend your mitt toward the incoming pitch. Go to the ball. Don't wait for it to come to you.

- If the pitch just misses the strike zone, catch it and move your mitt back into the strike zone in a single quick motion. The hand can be quicker than the eye. You will sometimes con the umpire into calling it a strike. (But first be *sure* you've caught the ball.)

Pointers for Catchers

- Your pitcher depends on you. Talk to him. Keep him steady and under your control. Pace him. Slow him down. Make him concentrate. Encourage him.

- Give your pitcher a good target. If he consistently misses the strike zone in one place, move your mitt to the opposite side. Make him focus on pitching to it.

- Most kids tend to pitch high and outside. Start them off with a low, inside target. (This is also a good pitch to the stronger hitters. It takes away some of their power.)

- Don't give signals on every pitch. Just let the pitcher throw hard and fast over the plate. He has enough on his mind as it is. The only signal you need, rarely, is for the change-up (and for an occasional pitchout).

- On all plays (except steals of any base), get your mask off and toss it far away where you won't step on it. (Why not on steals? Because you can't take the time.)

- Never leave home plate unguarded if there is a runner on base.

- Watch the runner crossing the plate, to see if he touches it. If not, you can appeal and he will be out.

- Be friendly with the umpire.
  - — Let him know your name.
  - — Smile at him.
  - — Talk to him (nicely).
  - — Don't argue (a surprised, hurt glance of disbelief is okay once in a while).

You may harbor doubts about his IQ and his eyesight, but treat him like Einstein with X-ray vision. He won't intentionally make calls in your favor, but (believe it or not), he is human. *It can't hurt.*

Throws by the Catcher

- Concentrate first on *accuracy*, then on speed. A hard, speedy throw does no good as it soars into the outfield.

- Throw standing up (not from a crouch). Look at your target. Get your balance. Take one step forward and throw overhand.

- *Never* make an unnecessary throw. Throw only if there is a chance to get the out.

- *Never* try to pick off a runner at first base. The odds are loaded against you. The chance of getting him out is nil, and the ball may end up being chased by your right fielder.

- Return the ball sharply and directly to the pitcher.
  - Throw it *to* him. Don't force him to scramble after poor throws. You'll tire him out.
  - Throw it on a line. Put some heat on it. Don't lob or arc it.

- Watch for the delayed steal (as you return the ball). Alert your infield to watch for it too. Fake a throw, and be prepared to throw if the runner goes.

- With a runner on third, step in front of the plate, look him back to the base, and zip the ball back to the pitcher. Or throw it hard and quick to third to catch him by surprise. Make sure you don't surprise your third baseman as well.

- With runners at first and third, you'll usually make no throw on a steal of second. What can you do?
  - Maybe gamble and throw if there is a really slow runner on first, with two out.
  - Maybe gamble and throw when the out is more important than preventing the run. Like when you have a two run lead in the last inning.
  - Maybe fake a throw and hope the runner on third breaks for the plate.
  - Or throw immediately to the third baseman, hoping to catch the runner on the basepath.

— Or fire the ball to the shortstop, who immediately guns it right back to you. (You'd better practice this one before trying it in a game.)

- When returning a wild pitch (with a runner at third), go back to the plate before you return the ball to the mound. Never throw it to the pitcher while the plate is unguarded.

The Pitch into the Dirt

- *Block it! Block it!*

  — Concentrate on blocking the ball. Don't worry about catching it.

  — Keep the ball in front of you at all costs. Don't let it get away.

  — Keep your eyes on the ball. Don't close your eyes.

  — Don't turn your head away. (Your mask won't protect the side of your face.)

  — If the ball is in front of you, drop to both knees and block it.

Block It

— If the ball is to the side, drop your body toward the ball. Land on your inside knee (the knee toward the plate).

— Curl your shoulder and upper body high around the ball (toward the plate). This keeps the ball in front of you.

— When you've got it blocked, relax your hands and pounce on the ball.

— "But," you ask, "what if there's nobody on base? Why bother?" Block it anyway. It's good practice; it's a tough move, and the more you do it, the better you'll be.

— Also, remember that on ball four, the batter can keep on going to second if the pitch gets away.

Making the Putout at Home

• On a *force* at home, stretch for the ball like a first baseman.

• If there's no force:

— Don't totally block the plate or the baseline if you don't already have the ball in your hand. This is an "obstruction" and the runner will automatically be called safe at home.

— Wait for the throw just one step in front of the plate.

— Stand with your left foot on the baseline. Let the runner have only the outside part of the basepath.

— Keep one eye on the ball and one eye on the runner. But *play the ball first.* Don't worry about the tag until you've got the ball.

Taking the Throw

— On a good throw, don't run forward. Wait for the ball in front of the plate.

• When you make the tag:

— *Concentrate on holding onto the ball.* Hold it in your bare hand, and protect it with your mitt. A two-handed tag keeps the ball from being knocked loose.

— Always expect and be ready for some kind of collision. Hold on to the ball even if you get whomped. It's part of the game.

— Keep your knees bent and flexible, to absorb the impact.

— On a sliding runner, collapse onto your right knee to cover the basepath as you make the tag.

— Always tag down low (Read the section on Tagging a Runner in Chapter 7.)

• If the runner dodges the tag but misses the plate, don't chase him. Wait there for him to come back, or appeal if he doesn't.

Tag Low, Hang onto that Ball

Fielding Bunts

- Field bunts with two hands. Scoop the ball into the mitt. Get control of the ball before you throw.

- The catcher should field all bunts he can reach. (*Except* with a runner on third, he stays at the plate to take the throw.)

- On a bunt along the first base line, step toward the mound

**Scoop the Bunt
Into the Mitt**

with the ball, so you don't have to throw over or around the runner.

Pop-Ups

- Locate the ball quickly.
- Toss your mask far away in the opposite direction.
- If there's a runner on base (especially third), be alert. He may tag up.

Intentional Walks

- In some leagues, the catcher must stand behind the plate on an intentional walk, until the pitcher releases the ball.
- If your league has this rule:
  - Stand straight up (don't crouch).
  - Hold your hands up and out away from the batter. This gives the pitcher his target.
  - Stand with your feet only about a foot apart, and be set to spring toward the ball.
  - Be prepared for a wild pitch. Some kids tend to throw the ball too high or too wide as they try to keep it away from the batter.
  - Tell the pitcher to throw at medium speed, on a direct line (don't throw a high arc).
  - Remember that the runners can steal during the intentional walk. Don't forget about them.

Catcher's Equipment

Be certain your equipment fits you well and that you have put it on correctly. It is designed to protect you from serious injury.

The Mask (with helmet) and Throat Protector: You must be able to see clearly in front and partially out the sides. Don't put it on too tightly, so you can get it off easily during the game.

The Mitt: It should be flexible, with a deep pocket and web, and a break toward the bottom. The ball should stay in the pocket and not pop out as you catch it.

The Chest Protector: Don't wear it too low. Adjust the straps so it will ride high and protect your collarbone. It should be a snug fit and not flop around (but not too tight).

The Shin Guards: These should be long enough so the flap covers the top half of your foot. They should not be too long, or they'll get in your way. Make sure the straps are tight and the buckles are on the outside of each leg.

The Protector Cup: *Never even think of catching without a cup.* This goes for practice as well as in a game. Wear it and you'll never know how important it was. Forget it and one day you'll find out how important it is. You don't know the meaning of *pain* until you take a shot in your tender spot. You don't want to know!

- You really should wear a cup at any position, not only as catcher.

- Always keep your equipment on between innings unless you're going to bat. Put it on again after you return to the dugout.

About Catchers

- The catcher is leader of his team. He is baseball's quarterback. Catchers, more than any other position, have gone on to become major league managers.

- *The Smartest Athlete Ever* (in any sport) was an American League catcher named Moe Berg.

  — Moe's IQ was around 200, but unfortunately so was his batting average. It was said that "Berg can speak 12 different languages, but he can't hit a curve ball in any of them."

  — Moe Berg was a genius. He graduated from Princeton and received a law degree at Columbia. In Japan, he made a speech to the legislature (in Japanese) and conversed with the emperor.

  — Albert Einstein taught him nuclear physics (Berg, that is—not the emperor). During World War II, Berg served as an American spy behind enemy lines. He uncovered important secret information about Germany's progress toward the atomic bomb.

- *The Most Memorable Play* by a catcher is one that Mickey Owen would rather forget.

  — The Dodgers led the Yankees 4-3 in Game four of the 1941 World Series. With two out in the ninth inning, Yankee batter Tommy Henrich swung at and missed a nasty curve ball for strike three. But the ball got away from Dodger catcher Mickey Owen. Under major league rules (not kids' baseball), the batter can run on a dropped third strike. Henrich made it safely to first base. The Yankees were still alive. They took advantage of Owen's gift, scoring four runs to win the game they had already lost.

- About that game, Yogi Berra would have said. "It ain't over until it's over."

Yogi Berra

Some Other "Berraisms"

When the wife of New York's mayor told him he looked "cool" in his summer suit, he replied, "Thanks, you don't look so hot yourself."

His opinion of Little League baseball: "It's good because it keeps the kids out of the house."

On a special ceremony in his honor: "I want to thank all of you who made this night necessary."

There never was a more popular player than Yogi. Everybody loved him. He was the outstanding catcher of his era, with 3 MVP awards and a fielding record of 148 consecutive errorless games.

11

Rules You Should Know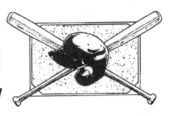

It's not enough to play the game. You'll enjoy it more and perform better if you know some of the basic rules.

This chapter is based on official Little League rules. Some local leagues have minor variations.

Fair Ball/Foul Ball

- The baselines are in fair territory.

- A ground ball is fair or foul depending where it actually *passes* first or third base. It doesn't matter if it started foul and then passed the base in fair territory, or vice versa.

- If a slow ground ball doesn't reach the base, it's fair or foul depending on where it comes to a stop.

— Infielders: Be sharp. Know the game situation. "Fair" or "foul" may be to your advantage. Let the ball roll or grab it when it's where you want it to be.

- A fly ball is fair or foul depending on the position of the *ball* (not the player) when it is touched.

Pitcher Eligibility

- A pitcher is limited to six innings in a week.
  — A week is Sunday to Saturday.
  — It counts as an inning as soon as one pitch is thrown.
  — Innings pitched in called games count toward the total.
- Once a pitcher is removed, he can't pitch again in the game.
- A pitcher must have three full days of rest after pitching four (or more) innings in a game.
- He must have one full day of rest after pitching three (or less) innings in a game.
- Not more than five pitchers can enter a game (except in case of injury).
- If a coach visits the pitcher three times in the same inning, the pitcher must come out.

When Does a Play End?

- Only the Umpire can call "Time out."
  — This happens all the time: The runner slides safely. He screams, "Time out." He steps off the base to

brush himself off. Hey, runner, get back! You can be tagged out.

— A player can *ask* for time out, but time is not out *until the umpire says so.*

- A play is not over until:

  — The runners have completely stopped at a base.

  — The pitcher is on the rubber with the ball.

  — The catcher is behind the plate, ready for the pitch.

Until *all three* happen, the ball is alive. This is when an alert runner can take off and steal the game. (That is the official Little League rule. Many local leagues have modified it.)

  — Find out what the rule is in your league and take advantage of it.

Batting Order

- Don't bat out of turn. Don't miss your turn at bat.

  — If you do miss your turn and you realize the mistake while the wrong batter is still up, tell your coach immediately. He can still correct the error and put you up. You then take the ball and strike count of the wrong batter.

  — If the wrong batter completes his turn at bat, the opposing coach can appeal (before the first pitch to the next batter). **If he appeals,** *you* are out, and the wrong batter's "at bat" is nullified. The next batter is the one who follows you in the batting order.

  — If the opposing coach **does not appeal** before the first pitch to the next batter, then nobody is out and the wrong batter's "at bat" is legalized. The game continues from that point. The next batter is the one who follows the wrong batter in the batting order.

Called Games

- The umpire can "call" a game for weather, lightning, darkness, or other good reasons.

- The called game does not count as a "regular game" if less than four full innings are completed, *unless* the home team is ahead or ties the score in the bottom of the fourth inning.

- *After four full innings*:
    - If the *visiting team is ahead* after a full inning, the visitors win.
    - If the score is *tied* at the end of a full inning, and the game is called during the next inning, it continues on another day from the exact point at which is was called.
    - If the *home team is ahead* at the end of a full inning and the game is called in the next inning before the home team completes its turn at bat, the entire incomplete inning is wiped out even if the visitors tied the score or took the lead. The home team would win by the score at the end of the last full inning.
    - One exception to the last rule: If the visitors score to take lead, and then the home team ties the score but can't finish the inning, the game continues on another day from that point.

Some Other Rules

- Every player on the team must (at least) bat once and play six outs in the field.

- When a batter is hit by a pitch, he is awarded first base, *except:*
    — If the ball was in the strike zone; or
    — If he swung at it; or
    — If he made no attempt to avoid being hit by the pitch.
  In any case, the ball is dead.

- After two strikes:
    — If the batter bunts foul, he is out.
    — If the catcher holds onto a foul tip, the batter is out.

12

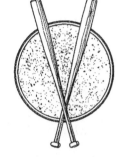

Nicknames

Many baseball stars had legendary nicknames. Here are some colorful ones:

"Babe" Ruth—**"The Bambino"**—**"The Sultan of Swat"** (no explanation needed here).

"The Big Train"—Walter Johnson (Washington Senator fastballer).

"Charlie Hustle"—Pete Rose (always hustling).

"Cool Papa" Bell—(Negro League superstar).

"Dazzy" Vance and **"Dizzy"** Dean (pitching wizards).

"The Duke of Flatbush"—Duke Snider (Brooklyn Dodgers played at Flatbush Avenue).

"The Flying Dutchman"—Honus Wagner (Pirates immortal of the early 1900s).

"The Fordham Flash"—Frankie Frisch (attended Fordham University).

"The Georgia Peach"—Ty Cobb (born in Georgia).

"The Glue"—Willie Stargell (he held the Pirates together).

"The Gray Eagle"—Tris Speaker (gray haired in his youth).

"Hammerin' Hank" Aaron (home run king).

"Home Run" Baker (home run king of the "dead ball" era, the early 1900s).

"The Iron Horse"—Lou Gehrig (played in 2,130 straight games).

The Georgia Peach—Ty Cobb

The Glue—Willie Stargell

"Joltin' Joe" Di Maggio—**"The Yankee Clipper"** (no explanation needed here, either).

"King Kong"—Charlie Keller (Joe's powerful outfield teammate).

"The Lip"—Leo Durocher (always arguing with umpires).

"Little Napoleon"—John McGraw (managed the Giants like a dictator).

"Louisiana Lightning"—Ron Guidry (Yankee pitcher from the bayou).

"Mr. October"—Reggie Jackson (greatest heroics were in the World Series).

"Old Reliable"—Tommy Henrich (Joe Di Maggio's other outfield teammate. Got the hits when really needed).

"Pee Wee" Reese (Dodger shortstop won a marbles championship as a kid).

"Pepper" Martin (sparkplug of the Cardinals "Gashouse Gang" of the 1930s).

"Pistol Pete" Reiser (Dodger speedster with a rifle arm).

"Poison" Brothers—**"Big Poison"** Paul Waner—**"Little Poison"** Lloyd Waner (Pirates' brother batting heroes).

"Satchel" Paige (Negro League ace. Possibly the greatest pitcher of all time).

"Say Hey Kid"—Willie Mays ("Say Hey" was his favorite expression).

"Scooter"—Phil Rizzuto (Holy Cow! What a Yankee shortstop).

"Shoeless Joe" Jackson (Crackerjack hitter, sadly involved in Black Sox scandal).

Pepper Martin—Leader of the Gashouse Gang

"The Splendid Splinter"—Ted Williams (tall and slender; the last .400 hitter).

"The Sweet Switcher"—Mickey Mantle (he batted both lefty and righty).

"Tom Terrific"—Tom Seaver (Mets and Reds pitcher; the All-American boy).

"Yogi" Berra (some said he looks like a Yogi, whatever that means).

The nicknames above are from bygone days.

Today you have:

"The Big Hurt"—Frank Thomas.

"Neon Deion" Sanders.

Can you think of any others?

13

The Brain Game

The game of baseball is only half physical. The other half is played between your ears.

You can be a good hitter or a good fielder on brawn alone. But you can never be a complete ballplayer unless you use your brain. *All the time!*

This means thinking; understanding and keeping your mind only on the game.

It also means controlling your emotions—don't let them control you.

- Always remember: Baseball is a *team game*. It takes all nine players pulling together to win.

- *Teamwork:* It's great to be a superhero. But if you only need a single to win the game, don't swing for the fences. The team comes first.

- *Team spirit:* Talk it up—from the dugout and from the field. Encourage your teammates. Keep the chatter alive.

- Never criticize your teammate. Believe me, he didn't strike out or drop that fly on purpose. He'd give his soul for another chance. If you chew him out or put him down, you'll hurt him deeply. You might even lose a friend.

- Constructive criticism is okay. You can show your teammate what he did wrong so that he'll improve. Just make sure he knows you're trying to help him. Smile. Take him aside and speak privately if you can.

- Keep your cool. If you strike out or muff that fly, don't get all shook up. Don't be ashamed if you gave it your best. It happens to everyone. Don't cry. Don't make excuses. Shake it off and play the game.

- If you did something great, don't brag about it. Let your play speak for itself. Nobody enjoys a blowhard.

- Know your opponents. Know their strengths and weaknesses. Where can you take advantage of them? Know their style of play and what to expect, so you won't be taken by surprise.

- Don't heckle your opponents. Don't curse them out or make fun of them (it's against Little League rules). Shake hands at the end of the game.

- On those wonderful occasions when the umpire and you don't quite see eye to eye:
    — Give him your best "you've got to be kidding" look.
    — Don't utter a single word. The wrong one can get you thrown out of the game.
    — Don't let it bother you. Laugh it off and get on with your game.
    — Remember: *The umpire is always right,* even when he's wrong.

- *Hustle:*
  — Don't walk when you can run.
  — Hustle to the ball. Hustle to your position. Hustle to the dugout.
  — Don't move lazily. Get the lead out.
  — Put some pep into your play.

- *Practice a lot.* Practice to correct your weaknesses. Practice to sharpen your skills. You can always do better.
  — Major leaguers never stop practicing. The greatest players practice the most.

- *Learn about the game:*
  — Learn the rules.
  — Understand strategies and why they make sense.
  — Read about baseball's colorful past: famous players, historic games, important records.
  — Follow the current pennant races. The more you know about baseball, the more you'll love to play it.

- *Never quit.* "It ain't over until it's over." The clock never runs out in baseball. You've always got a chance.

  It actually happened in our Little League championship game. The home team was losing 18-2 in the bottom of the fifth inning. They scored 17 runs in the last two innings and won, 19-18. Never quit. *Never!*

- *Have fun.* That's really why you're playing. You should look forward to coming to the ballpark. Enjoy the competition, the challenges, the successes, and even the failures. Enjoy the camaraderie of your teammates. Enjoy the game. Baseball should be a wonderful and rewarding experience for you.

14

Play with Pride

Playing with pride is the most important message of all. It means striving for excellence. It means having the strong feeling and desire within yourself to perform at the absolute best level you are capable of. It means wanting to be proud of yourself, knowing that you gave your best shot.

Winning the game may not be the most important thing in your life, but at the moment you're playing the game, wanting to win—the goal of winning—should be the most important thing (the only thing) on your mind.

When the game is on, all of your thoughts and energies should be focused on the field. Concentrate on what's going on! Be alert! Think! When you run the bases or field a ball or swing a bat, say to yourself that you are giving it the absolute maximum effort you can—and then force yourself to give an ounce or two more. You can do it!

If you know in your heart that you gave your best, then it doesn't matter if you struck out or muffed a grounder or lost the game, because you can truly say to yourself "I'm proud of how I played and of who I am."

Always "Play With Pride," not only on the ballfield, but in everything you do for the rest of your life. It will give you self-esteem and make you feel good about yourself. You will surely be a winner.

Dear Readers,

WRITE TO ME!
I'D LOVE TO HEAR FROM YOU.

Do you have any questions?
Any comments about the book or the game?
Any incidents you'd like to tell me about?
Want my opinion on something?

I'll personally answer as many of your letters as I can.
Be sure to tell me:
Your name
Your date of birth (including the year)
Which league you play in (if any)
If you're not a kid, what your role is (coach, parent, teacher, fan, etc.)
Important: Enclose a self-addressed, stamped return
envelope with your letter.
Hope I'll be hearing from you soon.

Jerry Kasoff
c/o Grand Slam Press, Inc.
2 Churchill Road
Englewood Cliffs, NJ 07632

Index

Share This Exciting Baseball Strategy and Skill Book with Your Friends

ORDER FORM

YES, I want ___ copies of *Baseball Just For Kids* at $12.95 each, plus $3 shipping per book. (New Jersey residents please include $.78 state sales tax.) Canadian orders must be accompanied by a postal money order in U.S. funds.

My check or money order for $_____ is enclosed.

Name _____ Phone _____

Address _____

City/State/Zip _____

☐ Visa ☐ MasterCard

Card # _____ Expires _____

Signature _____

Please make your check payable and return to:
Grand Slam Press, Inc.
2 Churchill Road
Englewood Cliffs, NJ 07632

Check your leading bookstore or call credit card orders to:
1-800-KIDS-499 (543-7499)